# In Search of an Equitable, Sustainable Globalization

## The Bittersweet Dilemma

A. COSKUN SAMLI

Q

QUORUM BOOKS
WESTPORT, CONNECTICUT • LONDON

**Library of Congress Cataloging-in-Publication Data**

Samli, A. Coskun.
    In search of an equitable, sustainable globalization : the bittersweet dilemma / A. Coskun Samli.
        p.   cm.
    Includes bibliographical references and index.
    ISBN 1–56720–512–7 (alk. paper)
    1. Globalization—Economic aspects   2. International economic integration.   3. Economic development   I. Title.

    HF1418.5.S26     2002
    337—dc21           2002023020

British Library Cataloguing in Publication Data is available.

Library of Congress Catalog Card Number: 2002023020
ISBN: 1–56720–512–7

First published in 2002

Quorum Books, 88 Post Road West, Westport, CT 06881
An imprint of Greenwood Publishing Group, Inc.
www.quorumbooks.com

Printed in the United States of America

The paper used in this book complies with the Permanent Paper Standard issued by the National Information Standards Organization (Z39.48–1984).

10 9 8 7 6 5 4 3 2 1

This book is dedicated to leaders of G7 countries.
Just remember, by helping emerging markets
you are helping yourself.

# Contents

# Preface

I planned to write something very different in this preface. However, as this book is being written, the most shocking event in my very long life took place on September 11, 2001. While the country and particularly the administration are feverishly looking for antiterrorist devices, plans or strategies, I maintain that proactively we must go to the root causes of the problems and not worry too much about the symptoms. This book, as a whole, may make a contribution in that direction.

Progress is the biggest enemy of violence. People see themselves and their environment making progress, people have hope for improvement, people who have much to lose will not resort to violence. Hopelessness, helplessness and desperation are very critical negative motives leading to violence. When the problems in explosive spots of the world—the Middle East, Northern Ireland, parts of Africa and so on—are not resolved and, in the process, the most powerful country in the world is perceived to be on the opposite side, there is much cause for concern about terrorism.

When the French Revolution or the Russian Revolution took place, not only had the gap between the rich and poor become too excessive, but also the poor felt helpless. Today the conditions are worse, since the poor can see on TV how the rich are living, while even worse gaps are prevailing between the rich and the poor.

It is not a matter of "trickle down" or "noblesse oblige" or "G7 meeting," but a G191 meeting is needed since there are that many countries in the world at the writing of this book. Not a top-down but a bottom-up orientation must be considered to approach the world's economic well-being. Global issues must be examined by all, not only a few rich countries. The problems of economic inequalities cannot be solved by the decisions of G7 countries only. All countries must be involved in this process.

Indeed, through globalization or interacting economically, politically with communication, with technology, with financial transactions and with the exchange of know-how, the world is in a position to go beyond a few privileged countries and bring all countries into the *global village*. That global village should be all-inclusive. All countries should be given an opportunity to benefit from globalization.

Globalization, without a doubt, is the most important tool to improve world economics. As UN Secretary General Kofi Annan stated, "Globalization has become the essence of modern life" (Annan 1999). As we improve the world's economic well-being, we will be able to get to the root cause of terrorism, which is essentially based on poverty. Hence, we will be able to eliminate the causes that create people who foment terrorism. Used properly, globalization can achieve such a noble cause.

This book deals with these issues. It makes a desperate attempt to make people understand that globalization without some compassion is likely to be disastrous in time. When Thomas Friedman (2000) writes about globalization in the form of the *winner takes all*, he puts his finger on the right button. If the winner takes all and if the capitalists from G7 are winning and taking it all, do we have a future? Just what will happen to the rest of the world?

We need not have a "winner takes all" attitude but a proportional representation in the benefit picture. When we deal with winner takes all, if you are a part of what I call in this book "have-mores," you are gambling and winning. But even if you lose, you can afford it because you are already a part of the "haves." On the other end of the spectrum, if you are part of the "have-nothings," what then, especially if you are forced to gamble and lose? But, you have nothing, so how can you lose more? Unchecked, globalization can lead to ruination of the poorest of the poor, and unfortunately, every day there are many more of them. The Center for Economic and Policy

Research reports that, during the past 20 years or so, economic growth rates fell across the whole group of 116 countries, life span has shortened and progress in reducing infant mortality has slowed down. (Hutchinson 2001).

Of course, not all of these are totally due to globalization, but the critical point is that globalization left alone will not do anything to counteract these experiences and, indeed, according to some, it is contributing to the worsening situation.

There appears to be no help from the rich countries. There is no international government or superpower looking after the best interests of the poor nations. There does not seem to be any relief from the widening gap between the haves and have-nots. Therefore, there are only two alternatives for poor nations. One is to stay out of it, isolate the country and hope to survive. This reactionary move is hardly realistic. Wanted or not, globalization will knock on the door anyway.

The second alternative is that the less-developed countries should not only participate in globalization but try to receive the most benefit from it. This book is written for that purpose. In a way, it is almost a self-help manual providing some ideas of protection against the ills of globalization while discussing some measures by which to benefit from it. With constantly increasing knowledge, Third World countries have a special opportunity to learn to participate in and benefit from globalization. The industrialized world has everything to gain if the developing countries can fully benefit from globalization.

This book has 14 chapters. The introduction where the general tone of the subject matter is presented is an attempt to elaborate on the "miracle of globalization." Chapter 1 presents a discussion of the details of globalization. It examines the four flows on which globalization is based and through which it expands itself. Chapter 2 deals with why globalization is needed and how it creates problems. Chapter 3 elaborates more on the key pluses of globalization. It particularly discusses the technology transfer process.

Chapter 4 discusses how the domestic digital divide that exists in the United States is becoming global, due in part to the globalization process. Chapter 5 examines just how some countries, some regions or some industries are being left behind. This is what is called marginalization. Chapter 6 presents a different point of view. It suggests that as some developing countries try to become more global, they resort to product piracy. A position is taken in this book that part of this piracy is helpful to get those economies going.

Chapter 7 discusses the rather unfriendly position that lending companies take toward Third World countries. They use a totally unsuitable one-size-fits-all orientation. Chapter 8 explores just how to become demarginalized. It argues that countries must demarginalize; otherwise their economies will deteriorate even further. Chapter 9 points out that in the absence of substantial outside help, countries that are being marginalized must develop their own defensive posture. The first step in this context is to develop an entrepreneurial atmosphere in the country.

Chapter 10 deals with what happens after the entrepreneurship activity. Third World countries, particularly companies in these countries, need to establish partnerships so they can enter the globalization process. Chapter 11 discusses expansion of the partnership arrangements. They become networks and trading blocs. These arrangements are essential to stop marginalization. Chapter 12 constructs a defense mechanism that is proactive enough to make a difference. It points out that the best defense is an offense. Chapter 13 points out the finer aspects of the strategic plan that generates a proactive defense mechanism. It explores how these plans can be successful.

Chapter 14 attempts to put all of the dimensions of the book into a proper perspective. It then explores much-needed research avenues for the future of a sustainable globalization.

## REFERENCES

Annan, Kofi (1999). "Pros and Cons of Globalization," Xinhua News Agency, September 16, 0218.

Friedman Thomas (2000). *The Lexus and the Olive Tree.* New York: Anchor Books.

Hutchinson, Martin (2001). "Globalization Benefits—A Mirage," United Press International, July 9, 8028.

# Acknowledgments

A book is never written in total isolation and without many people being involved in it directly or indirectly, and certainly this is no exception. I have benefited from many people's direct or indirect contributions. For many years I have lectured in several countries and in the United States and talked about wonderful aspects of technology transfer and, more recently, of globalization. However, when I visited Isik University in Istanbul, the Turkish lira plunged into oblivion. This was a major eye-opener. Another major influence is from Thomas Friedman, whose writings have made a major impact on me. Readers will see this throughout the pages of this book.

I am always grateful to my colleague, coauthor and friend of many years, Professor Joe Sirgy of Virginia Tech, for simply being there, arguing, interacting, discussing and sometimes disagreeing. His influence on my thinking is always profound. He always causes me to question and reevaluate.

My colleagues at the University of North Florida knowingly or unknowingly have been pulled into many discussions pertaining to many points of this book. Dr. Bruce Kavan, throughout our discussions and by exchanging ideas, was very helpful, although he may not even know it. Dr. Adel El-Ansary always has been a source of inspiration and ideas. Dr. Ronald Adams, through his concerns about business and society, made me think about many issues relating to business, the society and the world, which was always stimulating. My dean, Earle Traynham, and my department head, Jay Coleman, were kind enough to give me support and encouragement so that I could produce this volume just as I did my previous volumes. To a number of colleagues in two conferences before whom I presented some of my views, I am thankful. They interacted with me and gave me additional directions to modify my thinking.

This book could not have been written without the research help of two special people who are my graduate research assistants. Juraj Ciz is a very promising young man from the Slovak Republic who helped me put together some of the basic support materials for the first seven chapters. Phillippe Singer, a bright young Frenchman with great future, was very helpful in accumulating my research references for the remainder of the book. These two gentlemen were very enterprising, creative and helpful. Our secretaries, Susan Watts, Annette Driscoll and Alissa Downs, were always there when I needed help—which was rather often. Without them I could not function.

Hundreds of my students, both graduate and undergraduate, listened, reacted and argued about many points in this book. I owe them much. But, in the final analysis, I am the one who articulated these ideas.

Beverly Chapman gave me a helping hand in editing this book. As usual she was extremely helpful. My daughter, Ayla Samli, whether she liked it or not, listened to many of my ideas on the phone. To these and many others who over the years worked or interacted with me, I extend my deepest gratitude. As usual, this is an unusual and controversial book. But without controversy and debate, new and better ideas are not likely to surface. Therefore, I sincerely hope that it will raise some major issues and will make a difference. I am counting on it, and perhaps even a major part of the world is counting on it. People in these places who could make an impact, unfortunately, don't even know that this book is here. I certainly hope that this book will influence their thinking. I must make a statement here. I am solely responsible for this book and its contents. It was written with goodwill as well as many years of research and thinking behind it and certainly it is hoped that it will create an orientation toward goodwill and prosperity around the world.

# Introduction: The Meaning of Globalization

When somebody in Bangladesh can order consumer goods from the United States, it is a miracle. When Turks use Turkish-made automobiles, it is a miracle. Someone can send an e-mail message from Pakistan to the United States in a matter of seconds, which is a miracle. When the U.S. and Russian cosmonauts traveled into space and lived together for great lengths of time, this was a miracle. When computer aided design (CAD) makes apparel suitable to the consumers' desires, however varied they may be, it is a miracle. When a group of software experts from Bulgaria can communicate about technical matters with their counterparts in the United States and understand them perfectly well, it is a miracle. Thus, we must conclude that globalization presents many miracles.

We are living in miraculous times. The miracles cited above do not even begin to describe how fast we have advanced and how far we have come in terms of technology and globalization. However, the whole process has not stopped, it is simply accelerating. What we have experienced during the past quarter of a century is nothing in terms of what we are likely to learn and experience in the years to follow.

Technologies are developed and transferred. They accelerated the industrialization process that many countries experienced. Technology throughout this book is defined as the application of science to economic problems (Samli 1985). Such a definition brings the importance of technology into focus. Technological advances do not receive their value because of being a novelty or by simply being a means for doing away with the old tasks. Technology is very critical because it solves economic problems and enhances the quality of life in general.

Technological advances reach all aspects of life in all parts of the world. This implies that technologies throughout the world are transferable. They are transferred from innovators to imitators. When a technological development can be implemented successfully in another country, other than where it was originated, then it is truly transferred.

Without the transfer of technology, globalization cannot happen. But what about the nature and direction of technology transfers? Is it the power factor that stems from the accumulation of capital and in the hands of few, and does this economic might create a total imbalance in different countries? What is the outreach of globalization? Where will it end? Does it have to end? In order to at least partially understand these problems, we must take a brief look at the globalization process itself.

## GLOBALIZATION: A BRIEF HISTORY

Globalization is not quite the recent phenomenon that most people would think (Hale 1999). In the 19th century, globalization was well on its way. Technological breakthroughs such as the telegraph, railroad and steamship started the globalization process. The world shrank and economies converged (Hale 1999). The shrinking of the world and the convergence of world economies continued with capital flow, migration and information and technology flows driven by the constantly growing trade of goods and services. Evenett (1999, p. 16) makes the following inquiring statement: "Will the momentum of trade reform be sustained in agriculture and services sectors, which are critical to the future economic prospects of developing countries? Or will nations succumb to a growing backlash against reforms, retreating behind their borders, and squandering opportunities for growth?"

In the view of many, trade liberalization has benefited in many ways, but Evenett (1999) particularly identifies two key areas. First, when tariffs are lowered, relative prices change and resources are reallocated to certain production activities that raise national incomes.

And second, because trade economies adjust to technological innovation, to new production structures and to changing patterns of
competition, they may experience constant turbulence. Furthermore,
trade liberalization, it has been maintained, has been forcing companies to lower prices and challenge the already established monopoly
power within countries. It is further maintained that trade laberali-
zation can and has raised productivity in general. Since the trading
firms gain access to up-to-date capital equipment and high-quality
components and parts at lower prices (Evenett 1999), they produce
higher quality products more efficiently. In his words, Evenett (p. 23)
states that "productivity raises when businesses are exposed to de-
manding international clients and the best practices of overseas competitors."

Graham and Krugman (1991) maintain that there are at least four
major benefits of increased trade and foreign direct investment:

1. Enhances possibilities of specialization and comparative advantage. In
   other words, countries can specialize in types of industries that they feel
   most comfortable with and they are good in.
2. Increases the utilization of economies of scale since countries produce a
   narrower range of products. In other words, specialization leads to increased productivity. Large-scale production lowers costs.
3. Creates more competition and reduces the monopoly power of domestic
   producers. In other words, competition is more desirable than monopolies. Domestic monopolies are broken by international competition.
4. Facilitates expansion of positive externalities for improved production
   and technology transfer. In other words, infrastructures and other supportive conditions are developed.

Here foreign investments are considered separately. Agreements
such as the North American Free Trade Agreement (NAFTA) include
specific provisions regarding foreign direct investment. Most countries have adopted very favorable conditions and specific regulations
regarding foreign investments (Dell and Olson 1999).

Globalization has accelerated as the Internet has facilitated cost-
effective business-customer interaction. Over the Internet customers
require and gain access to a broad range of services such as corporate
information, product literature, on-line catalogs, order status and customer care (Taylor and Taylor 1999). All of these and other services

are continuing to improve the business customer interaction and are further facilitating the accelerating growth rate of globalization.

Finally, vast technological changes and an accelerating globalization process have jointly started a productivity boom. This technology-driven process and events have been drawing the whole world closer together (Pesek 1999).

## THE IMPACT OF GLOBALIZATION

The discussion thus far indicates that globalization is an ongoing and very powerful process. It is almost a natural occurrence and cannot be stopped. Its benefits are multitudinous. Without these benefits, global economic growth cannot take place, or at least cannot progress. However, the impact of globalization is abrupt and decisive. In that sense this impact is extremely cutting and for some it is dramatically negative. It is important to understand that globalization is not quite a zero-sum game, meaning that some people should not improve their economic status at the expense of others. However, it is not necessarily a win-win situation either. It is maintained here that globalization, under certain circumstances, not only is used as a zero-sum game, but can be a minus-sum game. In other words, while it is benefiting some in a very spectacular manner, it is also hurting alarmingly large groups in a very dramatic manner.

## THE SHAME OF PROGRESS

Perhaps one of the greatest fallacies of our times is to equate democracy and capitalism. Unfortunately these two are based on different common denominators. Democracy is based on one person, one vote, whereas capitalism is one dollar, one vote. It has been argued that accumulation of economic power through capitalism has been distorting the fairness of democracy (Samli 2001, 1992). This author has warned the Western intellectuals that capitalism is winning at the expense of democracy (Samli 2001).

Wilber (1998) quite aptly maintains that democracy in fact fights off the economic and social problems resulting from capitalism. He further maintains that as capitalism fueled the globalization of trade, it brought about the marginalization of countries. Since there are no established rules for globalization practices, nor are there any central agencies monitoring international trade patterns, global competition will continue to hurt some industries in developing countries. Hence, marginalization of certain industries and certain countries will continue and will even accelerate. Marginalization here means losing effectiveness and status and becoming regressive rather than progressive.

Capitalism has shown much success in producing large amounts of goods and services. This is truly a spectacular achievement. Capitalism has shown that investment globally, develops and accelerates world trade. Thus global investments are a key stimulant of world trade. This also truly is a spectacular achievement. And there are many more such achievements that can be listed. But capitalism has achieved this in a temporally and spatially uneven manner. While it made some countries or some people very rich, it did not accomplish the same feat across the board simultaneously. By the same token, capitalism has benefited different regions of the world very differently, again, not evenly or in a similar manner. The fact that capitalism proceeded in a very uneven manner among countries and regions is the shame of progress. While certain countries and certain regions have become dynamic centers of development, others struggle and stagnate. In time, in some cases, this process has reversed itself and thus some of the growing areas have stagnated and some of the stagnant ones have developed. This highly volatile process has become even more destructive with continuing booms and busts that have plagued capitalism everywhere. These noticeably accelerating economic imbalances are due to the globalization of capitalism. Perhaps Joseph Schumpeter's description of the dynamic process in economies needs to be remembered. Schumpeter (1934) described capitalism as *creative destruction*. As new products, new jobs, and new technologies are created, old products, old jobs and old technologies are destroyed. These sudden changes cause shock effects. Losing jobs, closing businesses and relocating plants constantly hurts families, economies and industries.

Whereas the creative destruction process of capitalism prevailed in the capitalist world all along, this situation has gotten worse in the global picture. The shame of progress in this book is referred to as "the devil in this orientation." Technology-driven globalization is constantly moving from labor-intensive to capital-intensive industries. This swift move is causing a near panic among people throughout the world who have been making a living by their toil for a prolonged period of time. The worst scenario in this orientation is that capital and economic power are concentrating in the hands of a few people or a few countries. By definition this concentration is marginalizing industries and economies further by making them weaker and ineffective.

## WE ARE NOT ALL EQUAL

The distribution of knowledge, as well as the level of industrial development, is not evenly distributed around the world. By definition, the developed countries have more capacity to absorb and hence use technological developments. These are the countries that have an accelerated globalization process. But there are also others who are not industrially developed. Thus, there is typically an industrial (or economic) divide. This divide is accelerated faster by the digital divide (or the technology divide). Hence the gap between the haves and have-nots is growing at an increasing pace. It is maintained here that these two divides are feeding off of each other and creating a negative synergy.

## THE GLOBAL DIVIDE

The economics literature is full of discussions, studies and analyses of what has been known as haves and have-nots. The "beggar thy neighbor" concept is very old. Unfortunately the economic divide has been with us perhaps since the beginning. There have always been statements such as "the rich are getting richer and the poor are getting poorer." The question is, how is the digital divide interacting with the economic divide? Exhibit I-1 illustrates some of the highlights of what has been happening as the globalization movement accelerates. Even though foreign direct investments (FDI) increased in a spectacular manner, the benefits do not appear to be shared fairly by the society. Indeed, if the average Gross Domestic Product (GDP) is increasing and still almost the same proportion of the population continues to make less than a dollar a day, then clearly the outcomes of FDI and increasing exports are benefiting only small select groups without making a dent in the preexisting poverty. In fact, globalization may be causing additional concerns. This concept of causing additional concerns is called here the global divide.

Statistics indicate, for instance, that income and output differences are widening between urban China and rural China or rural India or

**Exhibit I-1**
**Questions About Globalization**

- Eastern Europe and Central Asia
  - 1990-1998 FDI increased by 2500%.
  - 1990-1998 Percentage of population earning below one dollar a day increased by 3% to 5%.

- South Asia
  - 1990-1998 FDI increased by 500%; exports increased by 322%.
  - 1990-1998 Percentage of annual GDP growth remains stagnant at 5.9%, while 40% of the population is still earning less than one dollar a day.

- Sub-Saharan Africa
  - 1990-1998 FDI increased by 500%.
  - 1990-1998 46% of the population is still earning less than one dollar a day.

*Source: Business Week* (2001).

Africa. The income of urban China grew extremely fast during the late 1980s and 1990s, but the same experiences never took place in rural China or rural India, and the overall picture for the world worsened. These worsening pictures are attributed to technological changes and financial liberalization along with excessive population increases in poorer parts of the world. Additionally and very critically, the prices of goods and services exported from industrialized countries are going up, while the prices of products exported from low-income countries are not going up so fast (Wade 2001).

As different people, different businesses and different countries get closer and work together through globalization, the global divide also goes on. The global divide is the combination of the two subdivides, economic and digital. These two divides jointly and perhaps synergistically are causing the global divide, which is illustrated in Exhibit I-2. The exhibit first illustrates the economic dimension in the two extremes of developed and less developed countries. In between there are many developing countries, but part of the divide could also be applied here. By taking the two extremes, the exhibit illustrates this point. Vertically the matrix illustrates the technological competency dimension. The global divide here also is prominent. Some countries are technologically competent and others are not. This 2 × 2 matrix displays some dramatic developments that are likely to take place in the near future.

**Exhibit I-2**
**The Global Divide**

| | | Economic | |
|---|---|---|---|
| | | Developed | Less-Developed Countries |
| Technological | Technologically Competent | *Extra Power<br>*Highly Competitive<br>*Materialistic; Examples: USA, France, Japan, etc. | *Gaining Some Power<br>*Accelerating Development; Examples: Four Asian Tigers |
| | Technologically Incompetent | *Coasting<br>*Losing Some Power<br>*Exploring the Reversal of These Trends<br>*Looking for New Opportunities; Examples: Italy, Spain, etc. | *Decelerating Development<br>*Everything is Deteriorating<br>*The Country Does Not Show Much Vitality; Examples: Zambia, Sri Lanka |

The upper left quadrant illustrates the beginning of the global dichotomy. The countries that are developed and technologically competent are acquiring extra power. These countries are very competitive in the world markets and they are very materialistic. They are driven by greed. North America and West European countries are in this group.

Some of the less-developed countries that are managing to gain technological competency are illustrated in the upper right side of the matrix. These countries are gaining some power and accelerating their economic development; hence, they are preventing the technology divide from getting worse. Countries such as India and perhaps Malaysia are in this group.

The lower left quadrant indicates a unique situation. Economically developed countries that are not quite up to date in technological issues are still maintaining their leadership. They are simply coasting, but their economic development leadership may be in jeopardy. They are in search of finding ways to reverse the negative trend they are in or are looking for new opportunities to reinstate their leadership. Perhaps Switzerland and Italy are in this category.

Finally, the lower right quadrant indicates the worst-case scenario. The countries or companies that are not advanced economically, and also are not technologically competent, are facing a negative synergy of economic divide and digital divide simultaneously. Countries in South America, the Indian subcontinent and central Africa are all in this category. It is important to know the net effect of globalization by contrasting this group with the group that is in the upper left quadrant. Those countries that are economically advanced and technologically competent are economically benefiting incomparably more than the extreme opposite group. At this point the most-benefiting group from globalization is not necessarily exploiting the least-benefiting group, except the latter does not have any bargaining position. If the most-privileged wants to buy raw materials or supplies, it does not have to give a fair price or advantageous conditions to the least-privileged. Thus the least-privileged can be globalized and even improve its economy in absolute terms. However, in relative terms it is still being exploited and the gap between the two still grows.

The old dichotomy of haves and have-nots, as can be seen in our discussion, is giving way to two further extremes. Some of the haves are becoming have-mores and some of the have-nots are becoming have-nothings. The contrast between the two extremes is becoming alarmingly dramatic. Considering that there are more have-nothing countries than have-more countries, there is a critical danger of unfriendly encounters between the two groups. Even if such encounters can be avoided, having so many countries and so many people in the have-nothing category cannot be tolerated. Is it possible to create a situation of "soft landing" rather than "hard landing" for those who are hurt by globalization? Can the benefits of globalization be shared so that some of those who are likely to be hurt by it will be protected? Is there any possibility that those who stay out of globalization can be eased into it? These are among the many questions we will raise throughout this book.

## SUMMARY

In this introductory chapter we tried to identify the general parameters of this book. While technology-assisted globalization is performing economic miracles in some circles, it is also playing economic havoc in others. Thus, the old saying of "the rich are getting richer and the poor are getting poorer," or the gap between the haves and have-nots is widening, are giving way to a new development of have-mores and have-nothings. The gap between the have-mores and have-nothings is growing at an alarming rate. It is therefore necessary to find some "soft landing" alternatives for the current trends which, left unchecked, may lead to catastrophes. There must be some way to keep the have-nots from becoming have-nothings by learning to benefit from the technological revolution and (at least partially) the resultant globalization. This book explores those possibilities and also examines how these countries could protect themselves from being marginalized by globalization.

## REFERENCES

*Business Week* (2001). "Global Capitalism," January 29.

Dell, Champlin and Olson, Paulette (1999). "The Impact of Globalization on U.S. Labor Markets. Redefining the Debate," *Journal of Economic Issues*, June, 443–452.

Evenett, Simon J. (1999). "The World Trading System, The Road Ahead," *Finance and Development*, December, 22–28.

Graham, Eward M. and Krugman, Paul R. (1991). *Direct Investment in the United States*, Washington, D.C.: Institute for International Economics.

Hale, David (1999). "A Second Change," *Fortune*, November 22, 189–199.

Pesek, William Jr. (1999). "The Productivity Thing," *Barron's*, March 22, 24–28.

Samli, A. Coskun (1985). *Technology Transfer*. Westport, CT: Quorum Books.

Samli, A. Coskun (1992). *Social Responsibility in Marketing*. Westport, CT: Quorum Books.

Samli, A. Coskun (2001). *Empowering the American Consumer*. Westport, CT: Quorum Books.

Schumpeter, Joseph (1934). *The Theory of Economic Development*. Cambridge, Harvard University Press.

Taylor, Bart and Taylor, Dan (1999), "Under the Big Top at Telecom," *Communications News*, December, 86–89.

Wade, Robert (2001). "Global Inequality," *The Economist*, April, 72–74.

Wilber, Charles K. (1998). "Globalization and Democracy," *Journal of Economic Issues*, June, 465–470.

# Chapter 1

# Antecedents of Globalization

Crawford et al. (1999) maintain that the world's major economies, with few (if any) exceptions, will open their markets to competition. This will happen within ten years. But many "minor" economies have already opened their markets to competition. They are facing a phenomenal pressure to restructure their industries so that they can be a part of the almost unstoppable globalization process. To accomplish this, they need capital to improve their infrastructure and productivity. They need economies of scale to initiate competitive advantage in global markets and management to run this whole complicated process.

Could minor economies of the world enter into this activity and achieve the above elements to become players, if not major players, in the global arena? Perhaps this is possible, but it will call for a concerted effort of deliberate economic action. What has happened to many newly industrialized countries (NICs) perhaps can happen to all. But countries and companies must have a certain strategic thrust development process (STDP), as Kotler, Jatusripitak and Maesincee (1997) maintain. Strategic thrust economic development depends on first evaluating the nation's capability by evaluating competition in its internal and external environments. Internal environment analysis enables critical information for the policy makers to determine the country's strengths and weaknesses. External environ-

**Exhibit 1-1**
**Strategic Thrust Development Process (STDP)**

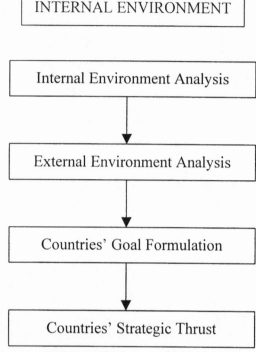

*Source:* Adapted and revised from Kotler et al. (1997).

ment analysis determines the country's opportunities and threats (Kotler et al. 1997). But such attempts need to be deliberately incorporated into a country's goal formulation. The latter is dependent on economic, social and political dimensions. If these three dimensions are not in congruence, the goals that are achievable and sustainable cannot materialize.

Finally, based on the environment analysis and the goal formulation, the country's strategic thrust can be established. The strategic thrust development process, as illustrated in Exhibit 1-1, is critical for less-developed countries to become newly industrialized countries. This was accomplished by the Four Tigers of Asia. Taiwan, Hong Kong, South Korea and Singapore are called the Four Tigers and are the real examples of what can be accomplished by developing and successfully implementing their own specific STDPs.

Unfortunately, most small countries and less-developed nations lack the discipline to go through such a four-stage process to develop a strategic thrust. Furthermore, many of them are engulfed by the ever-expanding globalization activity before having a chance to develop an STDP. Perhaps exploring how globalization came about will enable us to evaluate its characteristics and provide some direction to less-developed parts of the world. Globalization is a product of free movements of capital, information, goods and people. Thus, there are four flows.

## THE FOUR FLOWS OF GLOBALIZATION

There have been four major flows that particularly accelerated the globalization process during the past three decades: capital flow, information flow, technology flow and know-how flow. These flows have been catalysts for creativity and innovation in different parts of the world.

*Capital flow* started before globalization developed its current spectacular speed. Acceleration of capital flows globally made it possible not only to invest in many countries, but also to establish partnerships and joint ventures throughout the world. Organizations such as the International Monetary Fund and the World Bank particularly facilitated the capital flow from developed to developing countries.

Increased ease in the capital flow process in recent years made it possible for many international partnerships, joint ventures and strategic alliances, all of which further facilitated the globalization process. In many cases these options helped participating countries to develop their economies. But at the same time, ease in financial flow also accelerated consumer purchases of many luxury products that created a burden on some of the poorer economies. Similarly, some of the poorer countries, at the present time, are not capable of paying back the money they borrowed with interest.

With the emergence of the Internet and proliferating search engines, the *information flow* around the world has been most impressive. With such a flow industrialists, knowledge workers, sophisticated consumers and prospective buyers are all aware of the available choices and where they may go next. Information flow, as it becomes more dense and richer in terms of the variety of information, helps decision-makers all over the world, whether these are housewives bricklayers, nuclear physicists or CEOs of major companies. Although the information flow had a strong early beginning with the telegraph and telephone, nothing comes close to what has happened since 1995 with the emergence of the Internet. Different parts of the world have become much closer together.

Although the emphasis is on technology, the *technology flow* owes its start to basic product flow. As trade barriers were slowly lowered, more and more product trade started materializing. Among these products, those that are medium-tech and high-tech accelerated the need for and the flow of technology. Technology—the application of science to economic problems—has been transferred to different parts of the world. In fact it is the technology transfer from industrialized countries to newly industrialized countries that created NICs. When Japan gave technology to companies such as Emerson and Samsung, the South Korean economy started expanding. In return, both the Japanese and the Koreans transferred important technology to China. Similarly, automotive and computer technologies transferred to Malaysia from the United States. Each time such technological know-how is transferred, the recipient country gains decades of research, experimentation experience and knowledge. Such technological gains and knowledge spill over to other industries as well. The question in such cases still remains if the recipient country can pay back the profit requested by the sender of the technology.

Perhaps the most recent and significant of the four flows is the *know-how flow*. It represents the managerial or administrative skills moving from one country to the next. We suspect there will be much more of it in the near future. After the merger of Chrysler with Daimler Benz, a German CEO took over. Ford Motor Company has a CEO who is a Lebanese raised in Australia. The Turkish finance minister was the number-two man in the World Bank. Certainly such a flow of managerial know-how will further facilitate globalization and, at the same time, it is the aftermath of the globalization process.

After World War II, the "brain drain" became a phenomenon to study. Many less-developed countries provided highly skilled immigrants to more-developed countries. In recent years, such flows of people have accelerated. The Philippines supplied a large number of nurses and physicians. India is a major supplier of engineers and computer scientists. The People's Republic of China supplies a variety of scientists (Cheng and Yang 1998). As more and more of this human resource flow accelerated, a know-how flow at the managerial level started to emerge. This flow is not only from less-developed to developed countries, *but also from developed to developing countries as well*. This management know-how flow gave a special impetus to some of the larger global companies regarding their management and related performance in the world markets.

If these four flows continue and accelerate, this world will be a better place, but this statement is wishful thinking more than anything else. As was discussed in the Introduction, we are not all alike and hence all nations do not get the same benefits from globalization. In fact, many countries are left out of these four flows and have very little chance of receiving them in the future.

## THE POWER BASES OF THE FOUR FLOWS

Four developments in particular provided the impetus for the four flows: decentralization, deregulation, privatization and the development of cyberspace.

*Decentralization* has taken place in many parts of the world. Because of international mergers, acquisitions and other arrangements such as joint ventures, many companies have been forced to decentralize once multiple decision units emerged in the company. Changes in the political structures encouraged decentralization of corporate entities as power passed on to the private sector. However, such decentralization efforts also caused problems, such as duplication of management effort, ineffectiveness because some of the units are too small to be effective, inadequate and nonstandard systems used by different units, exercising inefficient localized practices or outdated processes that are used by different units and an infrastructure that is duplicated, among many others (Shah 1998). In order to remedy many of these problems, a concept coined "shared services" was initiated. This is an approach to alleviating the drawbacks of decentralization. Shared services are like a separate organization that consolidates the services that were formerly handled by individual business units during the predecentralization era. These consolidation service organizations share both staff and technological resources (Shah 1998). In other words, they could provide services for both management and staff and for other technological needs. Hence, decentralization has become a major activity in facilitating any one or all four of the flows discussed earlier.

As early as the 1950s, many countries tried to encourage international trade, particularly those countries that were devastated because of the war and needed to buy consumer goods as well as industrial goods. It was therefore necessary to accelerate export and import flows. Such acceleration could not be a reality unless some of the existing protectionist laws were repealed or revised. *Deregulation* received its international impetus through the elimination of international legal barriers to trade. However, it did not stop there. Domestically, governments reduced regulations that would hamper their nations' producers and reduce the countries' competitive advantage (Rabbior 1998). Additionally, increased deregulation facilitated foreign direct investments through international mergers (*The Banker* 1997).

Perhaps the most important of the power bases, *privatization* has allowed foreign investors to control some firms that were not private previously (*The Banker* 1997). Large numbers of foreign direct investments have indicated a strong trend toward globalization. Particularly U.S. and U.K. companies have been heavily involved in FDIs. It is argued that as an FDI takes place, it perpetuates itself because following the multinational enterprises that are expanding through FDIs, suppliers of goods and services, such as component producers or banks, also emerge. Furthermore, when firms invest abroad, their competitors also follow suit (*The Banker* 1997). However, much of the inflow and outflow of FDIs have been only in limited geographic areas, again leaving many underdeveloped areas of the world untouched, unaffected and stagnant.

One may ask a question such as "how wired is your country?" which measures the breadth and depth of its networks. With the development of cyberspace it has become possible to raise such questions and determine just how well a country is harvesting its knowledge. Since the creation of cyberspace, countries have developed information networks, so amassing and deploying knowledge possibilities have increased tremendously. But to use cyberspace effectively, countries must be well-wired and clearly more educated than ever before (Friedman 2000).

## TRADE LIBERALIZATION

Without being engaged in the riddle "which comes first, the chicken or the egg," it is critical to state that none of the four flows could have taken place without trade liberalization. And it is main-

tained that trade liberalization is the driving force behind globalization (Ghose 2000). Again, without becoming engaged in a discussion
of the benefits and ill effects of trade liberalization, the author notes
that virtually everyone in the metropolitan locations of Turkey has a
cell phone and over 14 percent have access to the Internet. Likewise,
someone in Pakistan can visit the Website of anything, anywhere in
the world. Furthermore, a Russian can order and purchase virtually
anything from anywhere in the world. There are hundreds of other
examples indicating the power of trade liberalization.

Trade liberalization, by working with spectacular improvements in
transportation worldwide, and communication/information technologies, becomes a more and more powerful factor causing globalization (Ghose 2000). Liberalization in the world trade came about
particularly after World War II. Many countries were not in good
shape to support their domestic economies and take care of the needs
of their populations. The need for industrial products, as well as many
more sophisticated consumer goods, overcame the traditional economic protectionism that prevailed prior to the war. Slowly, but
surely, more and more countries lowered their national barriers to
outside products, services, capital and information.

## THE CIRCULARITY OF GLOBALIZATION

The four major flows (capital, information, technology and know-
how) are all direct contributors to ever-increasing globalization.
These four flows have found their acceleration being due to decentralization, deregulation and privatization. But all of these forces feed
off of each other. In other words, as decentralization, deregulation
and privatization continue, the flow of capital, information, technology and know-how will be further accelerated. This acceleration results in more globalization, and this increased globalization further
influences decentralization, deregulation and privatization. Thus, a
very powerful circular movement is creating an upward spiral. Exhibit
1–2 illustrates this circularity. The question is: For how long will this
circularity continue, and what will be its aftermath? It must be also
emphasized that the four flows are simultaneously the cause and the
result of trade liberalization. Without the latter, globalization could
not become a reality. Thus, trade liberalization also has its own circularity since it is both the cause and the result of the four flows.

**Exhibit 1-2**
**The Circular Nature of Globalization**

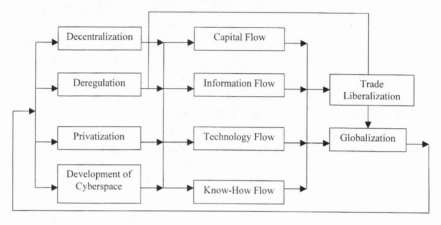

## SUMMARY

The chapter introduces the strategic thrust concept for a country. Economic development can be proactively pursued by the construction of a strategic thrust that may be quite different for each country. In this chapter, we emphasized the fact that globalization is the cause and the effect of four major flows: capital, information, technology and know-how. These four flows have become possible primarily due to four key developments during the late 1980s and 1990s: decentralization, deregulation, privatization and cyberspace development. It is maintained here that these developments and these flows are extremely interdependent. However, the outcome of globalization is impacting only certain parts of the world or only certain countries. Thus, there is a serious question about the sustainability of globalization.

## REFERENCES

*The Banker* (1997). "A World of Opportunities," OECD, August, 22–23.

Cheng, Lucie and Yang, Philip Q. (1998). "Global Interaction, Global Inequality and Migration of the Highly Trained to United States," *International Migration Review*, Fall, 626–645.

Crawford, Peter, Johnson, Kristen, Robb, James, and Sidebottom, Peter (1999). "Globalization of the Power and Light Industry," *McKinsey Quarterly*, Winter, 123–130.

Friedman, Thomas L. (2000). *The Lexus and the Olive Tree*. New York: Anchor Books.

Ghose, Ajit K. (2000). "Trade Liberalization, Employment and Global Inequality," *International Labor Review*, Autumn, 281–295.

Kotler, Philip, Jatusripitak, Somkid, and Maesincee, Suvit. (1997). *The Marketing of Nations*. New York: The Free Press.

Rabbior, Gary (1998). "Knowledge: The Key to Economic Success," *Canadian Banker*, January–February, 20–24.

Shah, Bhavesh (1998). "Shared Services: Is It For You?" *International Management*, September–October, 1–13.

# Chapter 2

# Why Globalization?

As stated in *Time International* (1999), globalization means that countries, economies, companies or people in general are coming closer together. This is not because they are forced to do so, but because they want to do so. In fact they want so much to come closer to others that they cannot help themselves. As worldwide communications get better, information, technology, people and financial flows move faster. The cultural assumptions and premises of democracy and free markets spread and become more readily accepted. This very attractive and almost irresistible globalization process becomes more widespread.

As was stated in chapter 1, the concept of flow lies behind this globalization process and has a special meaning of its own. It is perhaps singularly the most important catalyst for creativity and innovation. Throughout this book, it is posited that globalization can be the most important single factor to eliminate poverty and narrow the gap between the rich and the poor in the world.

## WHY INDEED?

Mainstream economic thought has some glowing promises regarding globalization. It maintains that globalization will lead to a widespread improvement in average incomes (Scott 2001). As this happens, economies of scale in larger markets will generate benefits that will help poor countries grow more rapidly than rich ones. Thus, mainstream economics takes a win-win perspective toward globalization. It further maintains that the importance of nation-states will fade away and the global village will grow as market integration and prosperity become more visible. In fact, some are much bolder and maintain that business, government and human relations will experience the vanishing borders of their complex relationships with each other (Annan 2000).

## THE MIRACLES OF THE PROCESS

By deregulating their domestic economies and opening up to global markets, Hong Kong, Singapore, Taiwan and South Korea have achieved standards of living as high as those of industrialized nations. It is globalization that is playing a key role in the rising UN Human Development Index (McCormick 2000).

Similarly, when Union Carbide opened a plant in India, it shared many years of research and experience with the Indians. A major technology transfer took place. When Fiat opened auto plants in Poland, or Ford opened auto plants in Malaysia, major transfers of funds, personnel and technology became a reality. This is how Koreans developed the VCR and TV technologies. Japan transferred the technology to Korea for a return of finished products produced at low costs primarily because of low labor costs. The critical point is that this miracle of technology transfer, which is a superforce that is further stimulating globalization, is continuing and is likely to continue indefinitely.

As globalization accelerates, perhaps one special force helps many countries to cope with this most difficult process, or to take advantage of globalization by being a part of it known as the knowledge organization. If countries that are having difficulty coping with globalization were to develop learning organizations, they could become part of the enormous power of globalization. This particular type of organization is in the process of emerging. The knowledge organization, or learning organization, supports sustainable competitive advantage—meaning that it can adjust to market changes quickly and can take advantage of emerging new market opportunities. This is critical for businesses in the present economic environment that is rapidly changing, highly complex and purports uncertainty. Thus, if knowledge organizations can yield sustainable competitive advantage—that is, the ability to compete in the world markets—those countries and companies that can create knowledge organization will benefit much more from globalization than those that cannot (Bennet and Bennet 2000).

## KNOWLEDGE ORGANIZATION AND CREATIVITY

Bennet and Bennet (2000) propose five organizational characteristics that support sustainable competitive advantage—all related to the flow of technology among the most advanced organizations as they globalize. Since the technology to access data, information and knowledge is growing very rapidly, organizations also are changing rapidly and much of the time becoming more and more globalized to take advantage of these technological advances. They become more specific in releasing the drivers of the forces that are and will challenge organizational survival. The five characteristics are connectivity, data information and knowledge, speed, access and digitization. A brief discussion of these will indicate the miracle of the globalization process, particularly among the technologically well-equipped companies and countries. Note that there are no major economic or digital divides among these countries. Therefore, these forces of globalization are likely to benefit all parties involved in this technological interchange.

*Connectivity* is the first major force. Technology has provided remarkably new ways of moving and transferring data, information and knowledge among individuals, organizations and governments in a very high level of accuracy, speed and flexibility. In the most remote parts of the world, anyone can talk to almost anyone in the world and exchange information at a mind-boggling speed (Bennet and Bennet 2000). As there is much more communication, the flow of information and ideas leads to better understanding and collaboration in solving problems and generating new ideas.

*Data, information and knowledge* are a progression. Without data there could not be information, and without information there could be no knowledge (Samli 1996). But most important, knowledge organizations have the groundwork for knowledge application as they globalize more and more. These organizations find powerful ways to use data information and knowledge (Bennet and Bennet 2000).

**Exhibit 2-1**
**Forces That Create Sustainable Competitive Advantage**

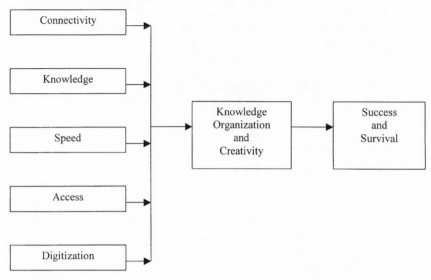

*Speed* in the movement of information, as well as goods and services, has put modern competitors in a more powerful position than ever before. These corporations create new ideas through virtual collaboration (Bennet and Bennet 2000).

*Access* is related to the above three features. Without it, connectivity, knowledge and speed do not have value. The organization must have access to these, and therefore it will maintain a leadership and competitive advantage.

*Digitization* of the economy is a recent phenomenon. It describes the overall movement to make maximum use of modern technology. This, in turn, creates new products and enhances the production efficiency. Thus, because of digitization, economies around the world are converging (Bennet and Bennet 2000).

As can be seen, these five forces are extremely valuable. As illustrated in Exhibit 2–1, they have generated the new knowledge organization. Such organizations thrive on stimulated creativity which, in turn, stimulates the firm's competitive advantage.

Considering the fact that with or without globalization, corporate entities are facing change, complexity and resultant uncertainty, it is obvious that these corporations, if they can, will pursue organizational intelligence pursuits. Hence they will more readily partake of globalization.

Particularly for some companies, globalization and related information and technology flows discussed in chapter 1 are extremely beneficial, to the point that they are irresistible. But as some companies get so strong, what happens to others? The jury is still out; there are points and counterpoints. McCormick (2000) presents what he names the ten myths of globalization. The following section presents these and some counterpoints. Although we accept, to a certain extent, responses to these myths, we also believe that the realities of globalization also show some support for these myths. To the extent that these myths reflect the realities, there are some very serious problems attached to globalization.

## MYTHS OR FACTS?

The conspiracy theory is presented as the first myth. Some people think that big companies are conspiring against smaller companies. But proponents of globalization see this to be a natural outcome of the dictates of the market. They say, after all, the market is free. In other words, consumers are calling the shots. By the same token, however, opponents would say that all consumers do not have equal economic power, and as some powerful consumers are empowering some other already very powerful consumers, there is no reason to think that the first myth may not be a myth after all.

The second myth is the theory of concentrating market power. Proponents of globalization would say that in order to survive in a global marketplace, big companies feel obligated to merge with other big companies. Even though GM, Ford and Toyota today control less than what GM controlled in the 1950s, this is only one industry. Opponents will take a look at the banking industry, for instance. A tremendous accumulation of economic power is in the making (Samli 2001).

The third myth is the evilness of the information technology. Proponents will maintain that information technology unleashes ideas, which are a prerequisite of learning, understanding and perhaps even of freedom. Opponents will say that it may lead to a generation of wrong or faulty information and hence clutter the facts. It also leads in the direction of creating unnecessary and wasteful products.

The fourth myth is that globalization is being performed by companies without any rules. Proponents will maintain that, sure, businesses are asking for rules, but where are they, and who is going to establish them? Opponents will say some businesses are asking for rules, but this does not deter others from having a picnic at the expense of the small companies and poor nations.

That globalization takes away jobs is the fifth myth. Proponents say yes, some labor-intensive jobs are gravitating toward developing parts of the world. But that is not bad. They are developing their economies that way. Opponents, however, maintain that most major jobs are becoming capital-intensive and thus poor countries are not benefiting at all.

The sixth myth states that globalization undermines cultural diversity. Proponents claim that because of globalization, more products representing various world cultures become available for purchase. Hence, there are now thousands of niche markets around the world. But opponents maintain that as capital-high-tech industries create jobs, they create a digital divide. Furthermore, allowing imitations and copies to emerge causes culture-related products to disappear.

That globalization lowers labor standards is the seventh myth. Proponents say that globalization is helping the labor standards by raising them. After all, foreign companies pay more than domestic companies pay in every country where they operate. But opponents respond that high pay is only for a few who are working for high-tech companies in those countries. And, furthermore, as the high-paying jobs move to less-developed countries, they are replaced by low-paying jobs.

Environmental destruction is the eighth myth. Globalization, it is claimed, is destroying the environment. Proponents take an interesting position. They think that as rising incomes and improving living standards take place, environmentally responsible attitudes will follow. However, although opponents of this position also like the idea of improving economic well-being, they do not believe it is sufficient. They would like to see more control over environmentally sensitive industries. They fear that poor countries may be too hungry for economic results and may therefore neglect the environment.

Myth number nine is that multinational corporations will flourish at the expense of smaller countries and smaller companies. Proponents of globalization would say, above all, there are only a few multinationals, and they are helping generate new products, new technology and new industries. Market access is made freer and easier for everyone. These conditions should benefit everyone. Opponents, on the other hand, will claim that global companies do not have equal access to many small local markets, therefore many local and regional markets are left behind and global companies are getting richer at the expense of these local firms or ignored poorer regions.

Finally, the tenth myth states that globalization widens the gap between rich and poor. Proponents would advocate that it is globalization that made the Four Tigers what they are today. According to them, by deregulating their domestic economies and opening them up to global markets, these Four Tigers achieved phenomenal economic growth. But opponents say that the gap between rich and poor is widening and there is no end in sight. Many other countries have not done nearly as well. Exhibit 2–2 presents a summary of these myths.

So if there is a solution, what is it? Nobody can argue with some of the miracles of globalization or the forces that are stimulating it. No one can deny how beneficial globalization is to some countries and some companies. Indeed, because of globalization, incomes are growing, but so is the income gap between rich and poor countries. There is a great divide in the global village (Scott 2001).

## DOES IT TAKE A GLOBAL VILLAGE?

Globalization is a mysterious process, but a fast-accelerating one. Even though it is causing a deepening in the great economic divide, globalization cannot be totally checked or controlled without having the global village do something about it (Nader 1999). Is it possible to reap the benefits of globalization, which are plentiful, without creating more hardship on poor countries that will be caused by deepening the great divide? This is an extremely important question. At this point, it appears that without having the global village to establish some regulations and some important parameters, it is not possible to control the harm globalization can cause.

It must be reiterated that despite its undeniable benefits, globalization can also cause much harm. This is because globalization is capitalism expanded, and all countries do not have equal opportunity to benefit from a worldwide capitalism that is expanding almost like a brushfire in the form of globalization. Friedman (2000) coins this as the "electronic herd." This herd can easily run over a country.

**Exhibit 2-2**
**Myths and Realities**

| Myths of Globalization | Responses | Realities |
|---|---|---|
| A conspiracy by big companies against smaller countries | Consumers are calling the shots | Unfortunately all consumers do not have equal power |
| Concentrating market power in the hands of a few large corporations | GM, Ford and Toyota control less than what GM controlled in the 1950s | That may be so, but market power concentration is a reality, e.g., banking |
| Globalization's evil tool is information technology | It was not tanks that broke Berlin Wall, it was ideas | Although IT is very important, along with good ideas also go many unnecessary and wasteful products |
| Globalization is companies without rules | Businesses want rules to serve people | Indeed some businesses might, but others are having a picnic |
| Globalization takes away jobs | Jobs are displaced, but this is not serious | As capital-intensive businesses replace labor-intensive ones, there is a huge problem |
| Globalization undermines cultural diversity | There is no average consumer and there are thousands of niche markets | By allowing imitations and copies, culture-related products are disappearing |
| Globalization lowers labor standards/makes slaves out of developing nations | It is raising labor standards | Only for those who are working for high-tech industries |
| Globalization is destroying the environment | Raising incomes and living standards will bring about responsible environmental attitude | Improving economic well being is the way |
| Multinational corporations flourish at the expense of smaller companies and consumers | Market access is made freer and easier for everyone | Indeed, on paper everyone has access, but who is benefiting at the expense of whom? |
| Widens the gap between rich and poor | Hong Kong, Singapore, Taiwan and South Korea have done very well | Many others are not doing well |

## LAISSEZ-FAIRE

Perhaps what makes capitalism work well in Central Europe or North America is its reasonably regulated version. The more regulated it is, the more stable it gets as shown in North European countries. Their economic stability, along with very high standards, has been a fact for over a century. Regulating capitalism is not quite acceptable by those who think it is against their freedom. However, it is critical to distinguish capitalism, which is an economic system, from freedom, or democracy, which is a political system. In fact, some authors think democracy is here to slow down the unfairness of capitalism.

However meager or powerful, the prevailing laws establish boundaries for capitalism. The problem with globalization as it stands is there are almost no political (or legal) boundaries. As globalization becomes more real and is unchecked, some countries and some companies become extremely rich, while local or national governments lose their power in the marginalization process. There certainly is a need for a legal framework for the globalization process so that global laws will not allow the marginalization process to move the have-nots to becoming have-nothings (Nader 1999). Otherwise without a common system of commercial rules and regulations, the Internet and the globalization process will diminish the importance of political borders and corresponding political entities (Gleckman and Carney 2000). The laissez-faire type of capitalism does not necessarily care who wins, who loses or if the game is reasonably equitable. That is why some people call it "lazy" faire (Samli 2001). Inequality being the starting point, it is questionable whether globalization will eliminate it. In fact, there is reasonable doubt that globalization can move have-nots to the position of haves, or simply can bridge the gap between the rich and the poor.

## INEQUALITY: THE STARTING POINT

Perhaps two key facts stand out the most when the history of capitalism is examined. First, capitalism has been extremely successful in producing very large amounts of goods and services; second, it performed, however, in a temporally and spatially uneven manner. Some countries and regions became dynamic centers of development, while others stagnated (Wilber 1998). This very critical difference can easily be traced to these countries' single and most powerful feature, inequality.

Digital divide, for instance, is a matter of skills. Those who are not exposed to computers do not have the mastery of the skills that will enable them to use computers beneficially. The skills are partially cultural and partially educational. Whatever their source, their presence or absence would make a difference in the economic road to prosperity.

As was mentioned at the beginning of this chapter, knowledge is related to performance, creativity and advancement. Once again, different countries (or peoples) have different knowledge levels. Regardless of the reasons why there are such differences in knowledge, the bottom line is that those who have less knowledge are handicapped. In fact with the information flow related to globalization, the knowledge gap is deepening. Thus, inequality is becoming more pronounced. However, globalization also is the only power at this time that can narrow the knowledge gap. This is particularly due to the efforts of both information providers and information receivers.

The economic divide that was mentioned in the Introduction is partially a function of a country's resources. Some countries have spectacular resources such as oil-rich soil, diamonds or gold. Others are rich in terms of sunshine and leisure opportunities. There are others that cannot even produce enough food to feed their own population. It is therefore clear that countries are not equal when their resources are compared.

If we can combine skills, knowledge and resources, we approximate peoples' or countries' capabilities. If countries are not equal in terms of skills, knowledge and resources, it is reasonable to realize that their inequality in capabilities is likely greater than the first three inequalities, since we assume capability is a function of skills, knowledge and resources. It is obvious that a country with less-than-adequate capabilities cannot possibly take advantage of globalization, nor can it protect itself from any adverse effects of globalization.

Indeed, these inequalities are painfully present. But even more worrisome is the fact that without any outside equalizing or stabilizing efforts, these inequalities are getting worse every day. Thus, one can claim that in its current form globalization cannot be sustained. It is essential to make it sustainable by sharing its benefits more equitably.

## IS THERE A REPORT CARD?

Without globalization, the Four Tigers, for example, could not have survived. However, is there a report card for globalization? Unfortunately not. Globalization, with a few exceptions, appears to be creating wealth at the micro level and creating hardship at the macro level. In other words, while a few are getting very rich, the majority are paying the price. Those who benefit immensely certainly would like to continue as is, and to truly micromanage countries accordingly. If there were no report card, why would we even question globalization? One can say this is what the markets of the world want and this is what they are getting. The question, of course, is where do we go from here?

## WHAT IS NEXT IN THIS MOST POWERFUL MOVEMENT?

If we take Wilber's comment seriously (1998, 465), that "democracy has fought the economic and social problems resulting from capitalism," some decisions need to be made. Just how do we separate capitalism and its powerful child, globalization, from democracy? Which should be the decisive choice, capitalism (globalization) or democracy? Are these truly opposing phenomena? Can they be reconciled? These are some very serious issues about which world leaders must be very concerned. Not only throughout this book will we address some of these issues, but clearly the world also will have to address them in the very near future and in a very passionate manner. Otherwise, the economic dichotomy of the rich and poor will spill over to political conditions as well.

## SUMMARY

Globalization is a shrinking world and many people, regardless of geographic distances, are interacting and working together toward an economic goal, which obviously is to make more money. But in the process, technologies are developing and are being transferred; data are becoming knowledge and shared among many; and creativity is stimulated incessantly, which is enhancing the market power or the competitive edge of many. This miraculous process is not standing still, but accelerating.

However, this acceleration process is leaving many, or most, behind. Those who are left behind are mostly weak and poor. They do not have equal skills to benefit from globalization as do their richer brethren. Furthermore, they lack knowledge, so as globalization brings about progress to those who are participating, those who are not participating regress. Clearly those who are not benefiting from globalization do not have the resources, natural and otherwise. A combination of skills, knowledge and resources equals capability. Those who are left behind are not capable of benefiting from the globalization process. We do not have a reliable absolute measure indicating who is winning, who is losing and by how much.

## REFERENCES

Annan, Kofi (2000). "Preparing for Life in a Global Village," *Presidents and Prime Ministers*, May, 27–32.

Bennet, Alex and Bennet, David (2000). "Characterizing the Next Generation Knowledge Organization," *Knowledge and Innovation*, October, 8–42.

Friedman, Thomas (2000). *The Lexus and the Olive Tree*. New York: Anchor Books.

Gleckman, Howard and Carney, Don (2000). "Watching Over the World Wide Web," *Business Week*, August 28, 195–196.

McCormick, Richard D. (2000). "10 Myths About Globalization: Modern Civilization Through Trade To All," *Vital Speeches*, November 15, 69–74.

Nader, Laura (1999). "Globalization of Law: ADR as Soft Technology," American Society of International Law, *Proceedings of the Annual Meeting*, Washington, 304–311.

Samli, A. Coskun (1996). *Information-Driven Marketing Decisions*. Westport, CT: Quorum Books.

Samli, A. Coskun (2001). *Empowering the American Consumer*. Westport, CT: Quorum Books.

Scott, Bruce R. (2001). "The Great Divide in the Global Village," *Foreign Affairs*, January–February, 160–171.

*Time International* (1999). February 1.

Wilber, Charles K. (1998). "Globalization and Democracy," *Journal of Economic Issues*, June, 465–470.

# Chapter 3

# The Pluses of Globalization

Friedman (2000) states that the driving force behind globalization is free market capitalism, which uses free trade and competition to create virtual rulers of the world markets. These very powerful capitalists make economies to flourish and be efficient. With the opening up of world markets, globalization has become a major force shaping both management theory and practice. Forces of globalization have been accelerating and, as such, are shaping policies and behaviors of nation-states as well as corporate entities all over the world (Rao 2001).

"In the last decade, global trade in goods and services has grown twice as fast as world output." (Griswold 1998, p. 30) This is an important statement indicating the importance of globalization. However, it does not reflect more than a fraction of the total outreach and impact of globalization activity. As was mentioned in the Introduction there are many more aspects to globalization than just stimulating trade. These aspects are more voluminous in terms of quantities and values. Furthermore, they influence our lives much more than simply finding, in growing proportions, consumer goods that are made or grown by workers in other countries. Globalization is an all-encompassing activity for many companies and countries. It is changing the way people communicate, the way people shop and, in some cases, even the way people think.

Ohmae (1990) wrote that national borders have little or nothing to do with real flows of industrial activity, which is changing rapidly. In chapter 1 we discussed different flows as antecedents of globalization. Of course globalization is both the cause and the outcome of the industrial flows.

These flows are creating cross-national cooperation among many partners. In the 21st century, information and knowledge, as opposed to military power, are the real sources of economic strength. While real flows of industrial activity may reduce the regulatory authorities of national governments, as well as undermining their borders, they are going strong, in fact accelerating. It is unclear how far this transformation will go (Atkinson 1999). Is it possible that many small and weaker nations may disappear and only a few unions of nations will remain?

National borders have little or nothing to do with the flows of industrial activity or of consumer goods. These flows do not quite follow the classic economic prediction that labor and material costs will become equalized and all participants will benefit from free trade. Nonetheless, opportunities continue to increase as a result of globalization.


## OPPORTUNITIES FOR CONSUMERS
## WORLDWIDE

Globalization has created spectacular opportunities for consumers worldwide. Exhibit 3–1 displays six of the important opportunities consumers are enjoying. First and perhaps foremost, improved global communication systems through advanced information technology (IT) and globalization are helping consumers. They are becoming more and more aware of available products and services not only in their neighborhood shopping centers and bazaars, but also everywhere else in the world. Such increased opportunities and choices by definition improve consumers' well-being everywhere.

Elimination of political barriers is creating ready access to world markets to buy a variety of products. These were not available when national and regional barriers to trade were in effect. Efforts of the General Agreement on Tariffs and Trade (GATT), and the World Trade Organization (WTO) have made it easier for goods and services to be traded around the world. Increased ease of trading in general makes products and services more accessible for average consumers.

Exhibit 3-1
International Consumer Opportunities Caused by Globalization

| Key Factors | Consumer Outcomes |
| --- | --- |
| o Improved global communication systems | Increased consumer awareness of available products and services |
| o Elimination of political barriers | Ready access to world markets to buy a variety of products |
| o Improved worldwide logistics | Ability to order and receive products in very short times |
| o Increased consumer sophistication | Greater need and desire for many new products |
| o Increased efficiency in production | Making higher quality and cheaper products |
| o Creating new designs and wider variety | Some consumers are getting some products that they did not dream of |

It also satisfies certain needs swiftly and takes care of emergencies, such as a sudden need for a special medicine.

By necessity, logistic systems worldwide are improving and making it possible to order and receive products quickly. The time between ordering and receipt of delivery is becoming shorter and shorter. Such increased efficiency in the delivery system provides faster and more efficient solutions to consumer problems around the world. It also passes reduced cost benefits on to consumers.

As the world gets smaller and consumers become more aware of opportunities, consumer sophistication is becoming sharper and heightened, and this creates greater need and desire for many new products. Not only do consumers around the world know the names of the brands and makers of the products, but they also have a good idea as to their specific features. Hence, they can decide what their needs are and which products or services will satisfy those needs.

As the suppliers of products and services face increasing demands, they improve their efficiency in production through economies of scale. This increased efficiency creates higher quality products at cheaper prices. Economies of scale, scope and speed help manufacturers around the globe to create more consumer value, by improving product quality, price and delivery.

Another development related to increased demand and improved productivity is creation of new products and greater varieties. In many parts of the world, consumers obtain and use products that they did not even dream of before. These products and their use not only create greater consumer value, but also stimulate consumers' imagination to improve their quality of life.


## INCREASED COMPETITION

Competition for consumer buying power around the world is increasing. Companies try to outdo each other, at least partially, by producing better products. Competition between Kodak and Fuji, Mercedes-Benz and BMW, Coca-Cola and Pepsi Cola, to name just a few, have led to improved products and services. It is doubtful that without such level and intensity of competition there could be so many new high-tech products that make life so much easier and enjoyable for so many.

Furthermore, accelerated innovation of new and better products promises almost the unexpected not only in information flow, transportation, apparel and housing, but also in medicine, the pharmaceutical industry and many other industries. Again, certainly at least in part, we owe competition and globalization much in these incessantly progressive developments.

So much for the products. What is happening in the services industries? When Andersen Consulting, McKenzie or A. C. Nielsen, to name just a few, help clients not only in one country, but all over the world, these clients, particularly those that are located in Third World countries, are exposed to the types of services they never experienced before. In fact, in many cases they could not have fathomed having equal opportunities, just as their West European and North American counterparts, to solve their managerial problems.

Perhaps even more than products, services are reaching out to the whole world and making a major difference because of the globalization process. In Chapter 1 this was referred to as know-how flow. Having access to, for instance, high-level consulting services certainly can make a difference in terms of the firm sharpening up its competitive capabilities. If global service flows can establish managerial superiority for the recipients, then the benefits of services flows are almost spectacular. Since developing countries face a very difficult problem of mastering the skills and knowledge of the newly emerging science-intensive industries, the services that help in that direction are extremely valuable (Kumar and Marg 2000). Thus, services are helping to transfer technologies successfully, among other benefits.

## TECHNOLOGY TRANSFER

We have defined technology as the application of science to economic problems. Technology transfer is defined as "transfer of knowledge, skill or flow of knowledge from one channel to another" (Kumar and Marg 2000). The role of technology and its transfer in economic development was discussed widely in the 1980s and 1990s (Samli 1985).

It is critical to realize that technology transfer is particularly important for Third World countries. Without technology they cannot possibly survive and support their ever-increasing populations, and without technology transfer they will not have certain technologies. Many countries in emerging world markets cannot possibly develop major technologies from scratch. But they are capable of adapting technologies, revising them and at times even improving them.

It is important also to point out that the role of technology can be seen differently as it fits the economy. Kumar and Marg (2000) state that technology is a dependent variable of the economy. In other words, as economic progress is achieved, there will also be more technology. They further maintain that without a modern economic system, countries could not have developed the technology to begin with. However, in the case of technology transfer, this is not quite the same. Technology is likely to come first in less-developed countries. It is the force that will jump-start the country's economy.

Exhibit 3–2 illustrates that whereas technology is a dependent variable in developed countries, economic development is the cause. However, the same technology, if it is transferred successfully, becomes the key independent variable that generates the economic development. Thus, technology plays a very different role in developed versus developing economies.

Just what industries need to be transferred and what is the transfer process? Emmanual (1983) articulated some of the earlier debates that are still not quite settled. He suggested that technology transfer is a shortcut to Third World development. Indeed, this author thinks it may be the only shortcut. Emmanual posited that regardless of whether the technology is transferred directly as it is purchased by the less-developed country (LDC), or indirectly perhaps through a multinational company or through foreign direct investment, superior capital-intensive technology is necessary for the shortcut, which the less-developed country can use to develop its economy.

**Exhibit 3-2**
**The Reversed Role of Technology**

**Industrialized Countries**                          **Less-Developed Countries**

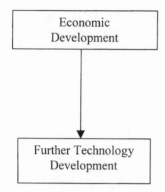

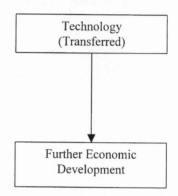

The discussion, then, went in the direction of distinguishing the "most appropriate technology" from the "most up-to-date technology." Emmanual (1983) and others suggested that if the less-developed country does not receive the most up-to-date technology, the gap between the haves and have-nots will deepen rather than being bridged. Others (Samli 1985), however, maintained that many developing countries are not capable of absorbing the most up-to-date technology and that they will make good progress with the most appropriate technology. Absorbing the most appropriate technology is much easier and hence may accelerate the maturing process of the recipient. The argument distinguishing the most up-to-date versus most appropriate technology is becoming less and less important. Because of globalization, most up-to-date technologies are becoming more comprehensible and applicable.

## THE PROCESS OF TECHNOLOGY TRANSFER

Whether it is the most up-to-date or most appropriate technology, the transference of it is difficult and problematic. This particular issue of technology transfer is illustrated in Exhibit 3–3.

As seen in Exhibit 3–3, there is always a sender and a receiver of the technology in question. The sender, if it wants to succeed, must know about the receiver's needs and capabilities. But the sender has its own needs regarding, say, how much of the technology it wants

**Exhibit 3-3**
**A Model of Technology Transfer**

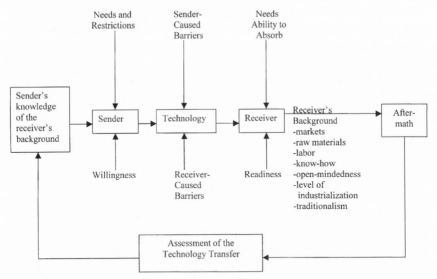

*Source:* Adapted and revised from Samli (1985).

to share with the receiver. Furthermore, the sender is restricted by certain governmental or political restrictions. When President Reagan did not want to share U.S. computer technology with the former Soviet Union, many computers were confiscated before they could be smuggled into Russia. It is also partially the sender's willingness to give away, sell or share the technology, which may be somewhat whimsical as well as materialistic. The Jewish industrialist may not wish to give his technology to Arabs. Or the sender may not wish to sell the technology unless he receives an exorbitant price.

As seen in Exhibit 3–3, there are barriers to successful transfer of technology, which can be sender-caused or receiver-caused. If the sender gives, sells or shares the technology without providing the proper setting for a successful transfer, the transfer process is bound to fail. For instance, when Union Carbide opened a factory in Bhopal, India, manned with Indian nationals exclusively, the company did not send safety technology knowledge. The outcome was some 2,000 deaths and 30,000 wounded people because of an unexpected explosion (Samli, Berkman and Grewal 1990).

Similarly, there are receiver-caused barriers. Some receivers may not have sufficient cultural openness to new ideas or processes. They may not have the educational level of understanding that is necessary to run a technology successfully. Industrially the receiver may not be advanced enough to use the technology to its best advantage. As a result, urbanization may not have taken place, and distributing the technology to a myriad of small rural communities may be a real problem. Similarly, the receiver may not have the infrastructure or the raw material to support the technology. These are all receiver-caused barriers.

If the barriers stage is past (Samli 1985), then still the receivers' needs and ability to absorb the technology are in serious question. Even if the technology is needed and the prospective receiver can absorb it, there may still be a question as to whether the receiver is ready for the technology. Taking care of the details of production, logistics, distribution, use and even exportation of the products of the transferred technology are critical issues that need to be evaluated individually, specifically and in great detail.

The receivers' needs and ability to absorb the technology may be the key areas the sender must examine carefully. Exhibit 3–3 explores the receivers' backgrounds. Over and beyond the receiver-caused barriers, the receivers' markets may be such that they need smaller, more durable, more energy efficient products. Thus the technology that is being transferred needs to be adjusted.

The presence of raw materials and quality labor has been mentioned. The necessary know-how must be provided by the sender, since the receiver is not likely to have it. Openmindedness and the level of industrialization, along with infrastructure, must be at the level and orientation that is required for the technology to succeed. Finally, the more traditional the receiver is, the more difficult it is to transfer the technology successfully (Samli 1985).

Finally, the aftermath of the technology transfer process must be evaluated. Both the sender and the receiver have a vital interest in that aftermath. It will provide feedback and the basis for future adjustments for both parties. With the development of the four flows the barriers to technology transfer are reduced if not completely eliminated.

## WHICH TECHNOLOGIES?

Although logic tells us that in the beginning the transferred technologies should be more centered on light industries, such as textiles or food processing (Kumar and Marg 2000), in reality it does not work quite that way. In many parts of the Third World, there are pockets of highly sophisticated technological development emerging, and these countries are becoming competent suppliers to industrialized countries. They are providing parts, components and semifinished products to companies of industrialized countries.

## CROSS-CULTURAL COOPERATION

It is clear that cross-cultural cooperation, in different forms, is necessary for this all-important technology transfer process. The necessary cross-cultural cooperation has taken at least three key forms: foreign direct investments, strategic alliances and joint ventures.

### Foreign Direct Investments and Partnerships

There are numerous ways technology can be transferred. With more than 5,000 foreign manufacturers—including such companies as Compaq, 3M, GlaxoSmithKline, Mitsubishi, Infonics and Nokia—Singapore has been open to foreign direct investments (Canniff 2000). These companies, by definition, carried technology to Singapore, and hence, the technology has been transferred successfully (Shao 1991).

Foreign direct investments are not quite as common or widely used as partnerships, joint ventures or other strategic alliances. This is partially due to many national governments' requirement of partnering with local firms. But it is also because multinational firms need to understand the local or national markets well and hence they find it necessary to partner with local firms.

Although partnerships are discussed in Chapter 9, it is important to point out that partnering with overseas businesses is difficult for both parties. Businesses in less-developed countries look at certain possible benefits that partners will provide, such as financial assets. At the same time, firms in the developed world look at certain specialties, such as unique competencies or special access to certain markets. Thus, functional and successful partnerships are not so easy to develop.

Even though FDIs are more desirable in terms of decisions, functions, control and other management activities, other forms of cross-cultural cooperation are common. In addition to partnerships, one of the most important forms of cross-cultural cooperation is strategic alliances.

## Strategic Alliances

In theory, international strategic alliances, which are collaborative ventures in the rapidly changing global economic picture, have some very distinct advantages. Among these are value creation, flexibility, lower costs and risks, strategic adaptability and competitive advantage (Ajami and Khambata 1991). But most of these distinct advantages remain only in theory. In practice, most alliances are not strategic, but convenient. The international company teams up with a national firm to enter a particular market, or a company wants to globalize and establishes a number of connections. Similarly, a firm that needs financial support finds a partner (Samli and Hill 1998). In all of these cases, the word "strategic" is misleading. Convenience alliances are much more common (Samli, Kaynak and Sharif 1996).

If strategic alliances are truly strategic, then the above-mentioned distinct advantages will be a reality. Truly strategic international corporate alliances will create value for both partners because they are synergistic. In other words, both parties have much to learn from each other, and together they can raise the performance of the organization to higher plateaus. This makes technology transfer not only easy, but also quite likely to improve the technology that was just transferred. Perhaps one of the most critical aspects of international strategic alliances is that both parties benefit equally. They learn together and improve overall performance, which is desirable.

## Joint Ventures

If for one reason or another the international company cannot achieve the desirable competitive advantage in certain international markets, it may establish a joint venture, another common vehicle of technology transfer. For instance, the government of Saudi Arabia motivated joint ventures and foreign investments to create niches in a highly competitive market (Abdulrahman and Ali 1991).

Joint ventures imply two parties getting together and starting a new activity. International partnering is a typical vehicle for technology transfer. Here there is no new corporate entity, nor is there much strategic implication. In order to enter the Turkish market, the international company finds a local partner and transfers the technology partially or fully.

Of the different technology transfer methods discussed, foreign direct investments are favored by investors. However, Harris (1998) calls this an imperialistic development. This is because today's globalization undermines the nation-state even though it originates from the state. This is due to the almost uncontrollable flow of capital, which enables international companies to concentrate on the world markets rather than national strategies. But as is implied by the use of the "imperialistic" concept, it is rather clear that the benefits of growth are not quite equitably distributed. The large capital inflows expose different national economies also to the possibility of large and sudden capital outflows (Korea 2000).

The other approaches—strategic alliances, joint ventures and partnerships—may not be so attractive to investors, but still are beneficial and at times may even be necessary. There will be much more on this issue in chapters 9 and 10.

It must be reiterated that the Asian Four Tigers—Hong Kong, South Korea, Taiwan and Singapore—have accomplished extremely favorable economic progress mainly based on technology transfer. One can say the same thing for Japan prior to the Four Tigers. Other giants are just about to show similar performances: among them are Brazil, Argentina, India and China.

One very important point is clear. Capital has more power than small national economies. As capital can generate benefits for itself, it will pressure for free trade to become more and more accepted. This power pressure definitely pushes for further globalization at the risk of undermining the authority of small national governments.

## ABOUT THE CULTURAL EXCHANGE

A major impact of globalization is on the cultures of participants. Cultural exchanges, acculturation and assimilation are very important far-reaching forces that play important roles in individuals' quality of life throughout the world. Traditionalists do not like to give up any part of their cultural heritage. People with more modern leanings like the idea of adopting parts of other cultures. This is a controversial and involved topic that needs to be explored thoroughly. However, in this book I have taken a culture-neutral position and am leaving this all-important discussion to another time and occasion. But the reader must realize that globalization, plus or minus, has a very pronounced impact on individual cultures and therefore on individual value systems.


## SUMMARY

Perhaps the most important activity related to globalization is technology transfer. Scientific developments, mostly in industrialized countries, lead to new technology development. These new technologies are transferred to other countries through direct investments, strategic alliances, joint ventures or simple partnerships. In some cases it could have taken a lifetime or even longer for the less-developed country to develop the technology on its own. But, through successful technology transfer, the less-developed country can save many years and immense amounts of resources if it is capable of carrying on the research at home without any foreign help, prior to the development of the technology in question. In fact, many newly industrialized countries could not have achieved their current status without successful technology transfer. Globalization creates technology transfer which, in turn, generates more globalization.


## REFERENCES

Abdulrahman, Y. Al-Aali and Ali, J. Abbas (1991). "U.S. Corporate Assessment of Joint Ventures in a Non-Western Country," *Journal of Global Marketing*, No. 1 and 2, 125–144.

Ajami, Riad and Khambata, Dara (1991). "Global Strategic Alliances: The New Transnationals," *Journal of Global Marketing*, No. 1 and 2, 55–68.

Atkinson, Glen (1999). "Developing Global Institutions: Lessons to be Learned from Regional Integration Experience," *Journal of Economic Issues*, June, 335–342.

Canniff, Mary (2000). "Eastern Promise," *Accountancy*, (Ireland), August, 10–12.

Emmanual, Arghiri (1983). *Appropriate or Underdeveloped Technology*. New York: John Wiley and Sons.

Friedman, Thomas L. (2000). *The Lexus and the Olive Tree*. New York: Anchor Books.

Griswold, Daniel T. (1998). "Blessings and Burdens of Globalization," *World and I*, April, 30–36.

Harris, Jerry (1998). "Globalization and the Technological Transformation of Capitalism," *Race and Class*, October, 21–32.

Korea Herald (2000). "Indonesia Striving to Ensure All Share in Globalization's Benefits," April 3, *Korea Herald Economic Review*.

Kumar, Naresh and Marg, K. S. Krishnan (2000). "Foreign Direct Investment and Technology Capabilities in the Developing Countries: A Review," *International Journal of Public Administration*, May–August, 1253–1261.

Ohmae, Kenichi (1990). *The Borderless World*. New York: HarperBusiness.

Rao, C. P. (2001). *Globalization and Its Managerial Implications*. Westport, CT: Quorum Books.

Samli, A. Coskun (1985). *Technology Transfer*. Westport, CT: Quorum Books.

Samli, A. Coskun, Berkman, Harold and Grewal, Dhruv (1990). "Managing Technology Safety Transfer," in T. M. Khalil and B. A. Bayraktar (eds.), *Management of Technology II*. Norcross, GA: Industrial Engineering and Management Press, 207–215.

Samli, A. Coskun and Hill, John (1998). *Marketing Globally: Planning and Practice*. Lincolnwood, IL: CNT Publishers.

Samli, A. Coskun, Kaynak, Erdener and Sharif, Haroon (1996). "Developing Strong International Corporate Alliances: Strategic Implications," *Journal of Euromarketing*, September, 23–36.

Shao, Alan T. (1991). "Joint Venture or Wholly-Own: Which Produces the Best Results in the Advertising Industry?" *Journal of Global Marketing*, No. 1 and 2, 107–124.

# Chapter 4

# Spreading Domestic Digital Divide

As the knowledge base of the world expands at a very fast pace, the gaps between those who have access to knowledge and those who do not gets wider. The world is becoming a more complex place to live. Some can take advantage of this complexity and others are stifled by it.

It is estimated that more than 60 percent of the world's online population resides outside the United States (Ploskina 1999). However, another study points out that 88 percent of all Internet users live in industrialized countries. But these industrialized countries account for only 15 percent of the world's population. Thus it is estimated that 98 percent of Asians, 98 percent of Latin Americans and 99.5 percent of Africans are not connected to the Internet (Thyfault 2001).

Samli (2001) states that in a democracy individuals have equal legal rights. Therefore, individuals are not to be discriminated against, and in the eyes of the law, all citizens are equal. Democracy is enforced by government intervention if necessary. But Samli (2001) also states that there are powerful influences in societies with antigovernment intervention sentiments. These influences try to eliminate, or at least reduce, government intervention to enforce democracy. Hence, governments intervene less and less. As a result, those consumers that are somewhat handicapped continually become worse off. Among these consumer groups are frail consumers, minorities, elderly, at-risk youth and the less educated (Samli 2001). Unless governments help these groups by providing them with protection, education and information, the relative status of these groups gets even worse. Third World countries are influenced by the industrialized world and cannot completely protect themselves.

What happens if these people do not live in a democracy? It is maintained here that things get worse.

## THE INFORMATION SOCIETY AND UNINFORMED PEOPLE

Naisbitt (1982, p. 37) stated that "we are moving from the specialist who is soon obsolete to the generalist who can adapt." Drucker (1992) commented that the quickest way for a person living in a developed society to make a decent living used to be just to become a semiskilled machine operator. But this is no longer the case. In recent times, if the same person wants to make a middle-class living, he or she will have to learn and accumulate knowledge. Salaries for semiskilled blue-collar workers in the United States have been stagnant for almost two decades. This is partly due to automation and partly to relocation of factories south of the border. Becoming a knowledge worker requires more training than necessary for semiskilled blue-collar work. Those who cannot acquire the skills fall into the cracks of the digital divide.

As early as 1982, when Naisbitt posited that the United States is moving from being an industrial society to an information society, he was right. Drucker (1999) talked about the most important group of people emerging in today's society as being knowledge workers. If the society is a learning society itself, then it will make the opportunities for becoming a knowledge worker plentiful and accessible to many. However, everyone cannot become a knowledge worker. At this time, the opportunities are limited, and accessibility for individuals to acquire information is not as easy as Drucker envisioned the situation. (Samli 2001).

Without a doubt, information is becoming the most important asset. Hence, with improved education, individuals have a better chance of landing good jobs and they are likely to perform better in those jobs (Samli 2001). If this statement were to be expanded into a society, then those societies that are progressive and are learning soci-

**Exhibit 4-1**
**Economic Fate of the Uninformed**

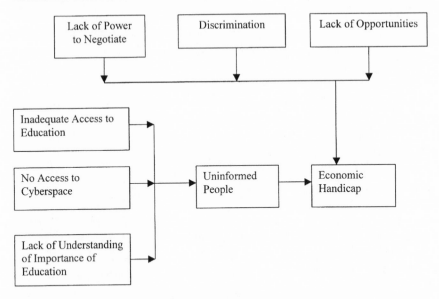

eties will advance much faster than those that are mostly composed of the uninformed.

The adjective "uninformed" has a strong connotation here. There are those who do not know, but perhaps are trying to learn; and there are those who do not know that they do not know. They do not understand the importance of education. In many less-developed countries, because of the previous economic divide, there are large numbers of people in that category. Exhibit 4–1 illustrates the fate of these people who may be the majority in some Third World countries. The key point in the exhibit is that not being informed about the importance of education creates an economic handicap. In many parts of the Middle East, Asia, Africa and Latin America, either because of poverty or because of certain cultural values, education is not emphasized. But those who are not educated find themselves in a vicious cycle. Because they are not educated, they lack opportunities for advancement, and because they have no opportunities, they remain uneducated.

Certain groups of people and certain countries that are economically handicapped find out that they do not have the power to negotiate, they do not really have great opportunities for improvement and, hence, they are discriminated against. Thus the economic divide continues and deepens.

What is alarming is the statement made by Mazrui and Mazrui (2001, p. 52): "Literacy as a source of empowerment has shifted from the print to the computer medium. There is a lingering danger that cyber space will solidify the gap between the haves and have-nots."

It must be reiterated that despite reasonable performance of the American economy since the mid-1980s, the gap between the rich and the poor has widened (Samli 2001). If American capitalism does not perform well in the domestic United States where there are some checks and balances, it will likely to go rampant globally where there are no checks and balances. Global markets today can be compared to open seas during the Middle Ages, which were full of pirates. Today piracy is illegal in open seas, but in some cases it appears to be ongoing in world markets. Friedman (2000) called this "the electronic herd." This is what was meant in the Introduction when it was stated that the economic divide is interacting with the digital divide. If the two create a negative synergy, then many countries move from being have-nots to becoming have-nothings.

Exhibit 4–2 illustrates this point in more detail. The United States, Canada and Scandinavian countries, among others, are doing well economically, and they are also at the winning end of the digital activity. They are on their way to becoming have-mores and have a brilliant future if they manage to continue in the present manner. However, there are those who have done well economically, but their digital status is not commensurate with their economic status. Italy, Spain and maybe Switzerland may be considered at that point. They are still in the have group and are likely to have a good future.

There are many countries that have not accomplished economic well-being, but are making significant progress in the cyberspace era. China and India are in this category. They are have-nots, but due to their advances in information technology, there is a possibility for future progress. Finally, countries such as Sierra Leone and Sri Lanka are not only economically poor, but their digital status is also negative. Hence they are countries moving in the direction of have-nothings. They have a pretty dismal future unless some miraculous development takes place. Miracles in real life do not take place, and there are many countries that are on this road of no return. They are getting worse, and the globalization process is accelerating their neg-

**Exhibit 4-2**
**Status of Countries in the Twenty-First Century**

| Economic Status | Digital Status | Country Category | Future |
|---|---|---|---|
| Positive | Positive | Have-more | Brilliant |
| Positive | Negative | Have | Good |
| Negative | Positive | Have-not | Possible |
| Negative | Negative | Have-nothing | Dismal |

ative journey. Thus, these countries are paying for their lack of information. That payment is becoming more and more costly.

## ACCESS TO INFORMATION IS NOT FREE

India holds a quarter of all of the world's poor; half of the Indian population is illiterate. In general the rate of illiteracy is higher for the poor (*Far Eastern Economic Review* 2001). In the United States, if a person can read, that person is able to obtain much information in cheap newspapers. Information is easy to obtain, and access to information is plentiful. Before worrying about the digital divide, India must worry about the hunger divide. In fact, the existing digital divide does not cause the persistent hard-core poverty in that country, but makes it worse.

Even though African Americans are getting hooked up with the Internet, they are lagging further and further behind whites (Vaas 2000). Governments must address the problem of digital divide or the lack of information by better educating citizens and developing better infrastructures. But this does not mean that the private sector does not have any responsibility. Since the digital divide at home is spreading around the world at an accelerating pace, the private sector must take a more active role in extending the opportunities that are provided by information technology to the poor and disadvantaged of the world (Hoffman 2000). In fact, access to information for those countries who are have-nots or have-nothings is very costly.

Exhibit 4–3 illustrates the major hurdles that an economically less-developed country has to overcome to become an information society where the society is progressive and its population has equal access to information. This state of affairs is not automatic. Without some deliberate action on the part of the government and the private sector simultaneously, it may never happen.

If ideas and values that originate in developed countries and reflect Western culture were to become dominant in developing countries, they might come into conflict with the values of local communities and traditions. Hence, creation of knowledge locally is desirable so that more orderly development within the constraints of the local culture can occur (Sydness 2000). This may be desirable, but it is also very difficult to achieve. Although Exhibit 4–3 gives the correct picture, it also demonstrates the heavy cost of becoming an information society. As illustrated by the diagram, unless the hunger divide is taken care of, there will be no economic progress. If hunger and economic handicaps are to be resolved, then both public and private sectors will have to collaborate. The public sector will need to improve education and develop an infrastructure to disseminate information. The private sector will have to spread the benefits of becoming an information society equitably. Could this be possible? These issues are addressed in more detail in chapters 8 and 9.

## DE FACTO MOVEMENT OF THE INDUSTRY

It is curious that advances in information technology have created a major mobility in the industry. As information technology moves around, industrial production activities start relocating. Preceding the information flow, industries go where there is information but wages are not too high. By doing so, they create a void at home, as well as a discrepancy abroad.

The industries that move from the continental United States to south of the border, or elsewhere in the world, are high-wage industries. Those good jobs for the blue-collar workers are permanently gone. The blue-collar workers who remain at home become hamburger flippers. Their spouses now start working, their families break down and they make perhaps one-third of what they were making before the industry relocated. As industries relocate, even though they

**Exhibit 4-3**
**From Less-Developed to Information Society**

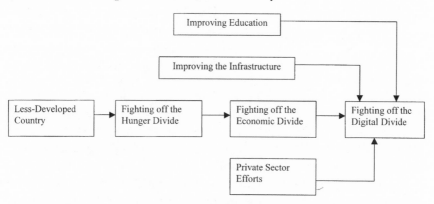

pay significantly less for the labor than they did before, the payments to select informed workers are noticeably out of line in regard to the going rates in the country. Hence, the relocated industries create a discrepancy that has important ramifications. It further distorts the already distorted distribution of income in that country.

One additional area that is not discussed in great detail in this book is environmental responsibilities. As American laws become stricter regarding water, air and soil protection, American companies seek refuge in countries where such laws do not exist and hence, pollution, on top of economic poverty, becomes a very critical issue because of globalization. Thus, relocating industries creates a lot of problems in both the old and new locations. If everyone does not have access to these good jobs and relatively high salaries, what then?

## PEOPLE ARE NOT CREATED EQUAL

At the outset of the third millennium, the United States, Western and North European countries and a few others are enjoying rising prosperity. However, simultaneously about half of the world's population is trying to survive on $3.00 or less a day ("A Great Leap" 2000).

In discussing the problems of the consumer, Samli (2001) points out that some consumers are frail or weak and need help. He distinguishes five groups of such consumers: frail, minority, elderly, at-risk youth and less educated. All of these groups cannot learn or master new skills at the same rate. Each group has its own handicaps. Those that are truly frail, perhaps somewhat mentally slow and the elderly may never learn the skills needed to take advantage of the transplanted technology or get jobs with foreign direct investments. Since people are not born with the same potential, some will get ahead much faster than others. If the population and economic opportunities are so diversified in the United States, it is easy to see how much worse it could be in India, Pakistan and some African countries.

This inequality is accentuated by a number of external forces in the United States. Among these are deteriorating inner-city schools, the lack of support for schools, the lack of properly prepared teachers and inadequate exposure to information technology.

Deteriorating inner-city schools is a self-fulfilling prophecy. Those who need schooling the most in our society receive the least. Inner-city schools do not get enough support, and those youth who live there receive less than a mediocre education.

In general, and very strangely, instead of supporting public schools that would provide equal opportunity for all, there is a tendency in the United States to take money away from public schools and give vouchers for some youth to attend private schools. These private schools are not scrutinized, accredited or controlled. This whole process is based on a questionable premise without a foundation that claims that private is better than public. Such capital-related propaganda sends signals overseas that are misleading.

Teachers in the United States make less than the police, but neither group makes much money. However, without adequately prepared teachers, the youth cannot be educated. Without education they cannot develop skills or acquire new knowledge. Again, the American approach may be taken wrongly in many emerging countries.

The at-risk or frail population has much less exposure to information technology. Neither in the schools that they attend nor in their private quarters are there enough computers and adequate instruction.

As can be seen, the American picture illustrates that not only are human beings not born equal, but also they do not exactly have equal opportunity in today's economy. Thus, through natural and man-made causes, the digital divide exists and accelerates. If it were not so bad in the continental United States, it would be hard to imagine what it may be like in many poorer and overpopulated countries. On top of the alarming inequalities and class discriminations around the world, the U.S. digital divide is expanding around the world, partly by the United States being an example for these countries to follow and partially by FDIs in these countries by American firms.

In the United States in recent years there has been much discussion about child labor and sweatshops. Unfortunately these two factors of production are a reality in Third World countries as globalization has become widespread. Children producing soccer balls and sweatshops in Mexico producing American apparel are common occurrences. They certainly do not help the global digital divide. They make it worse.

## CLEANING UP THE HOME FRONT

If the domestic digital divide is not getting better, if in fact it is getting worse, would it make the global digital divide better or worse? From our discussion throughout this book, it may be argued that the domestic digital divide in developed countries creates even worse digital divides in less-developed countries. This almost makes an argument against global business, but not quite. If globalization is not an outcome of the home-front digital divide and if efforts are made to close this divide, then globalization may not accelerate or accentuate the global digital divide.

A Digital Divide Network was created by a directive from President Bill Clinton. He stated that America would have a one-stop shop to understand our progress in every community. Attempts such as the Digital Divide Network can globally improve the situation before it gets worse. There are many corporate initiatives in this direction by companies such as Intel, Microsoft and AT&T (Anthony 2000). Unless efforts are made to stop it, it is easy to unwittingly export the digital divide as we globalize. Such negative exporting activity, no doubt, will come back to haunt us.

## SUMMARY

This chapter argues that, unchecked, the digital divide will spread globally. This is so because those who are in a position to use information technology are much better off than those who are not. This gap or digital divide becomes worse and worse. The more unfortunate part of this situation is that the cost of becoming informed for those who are not quite informed is greater than the cost of being informed. And yet, without information, more than half of the world's population is already doomed to a stagnant quality of life. It is maintained in this chapter that the United States, without improving the digital divide at home, cannot do a great job of globalization without enhancing the global digital divide. As United States companies invest, partner or engage in other types of globalization in Third World countries, they accelerate the global digital divide. If the industrial world is contributing to the acceleration of the global digital divide, the world will be in worse shape than before the globalization process became so powerful.

## REFERENCES

Anthony, Robert (2000). "The Digital Divide Network," *Black Enterprise*, June, 11, 80.

Drucker, Peter F. (1992). *Managing for the Future*. New York: Truman Talley Books.

Drucker, Peter F. (1999). *Management Challenges for the 21st Century*. New York: HarperBusiness.

*Far Eastern Economic Review* (2001). "The Digital Divide," April 12, 6–8.

Friedman, Thomas (2000). *The Lexus and the Olive Tree*. New York: Anchor Books.

"A Great Leap" (2000). *Time International*, January 31, 42–47.

Hoffman, Thomas (2000). "Leaders: Education Key to Bridging Digital Divide," *Computer World*, September 11, 14–16.

Mazrui, Ali and Mazrui, Alamin (2001). "The Digital Revolution and Reformation," *Harvard International Review*, Spring, 52–57.

Naisbitt, John (1982). *Megatrends*. New York: Warner Books.

Ploskina, Brian (1999). "Globalizing e-Business Can Invite a World of Pain," *Industry Trend or Event*, October 6, 4, 17, 30.

Samli, A. Coskun (2001). *Empowering the American Consumer*. Westport, CT: Quorum Books.

Sydness, Anne Kristin (2001). "ICT Examples in Developing Countries," *Presidents and Prime Ministers*, July, 4–6.

Thyfault, Mary E. (2001). "Global Opportunities," *Information Week*, March 26, 65–70.

Vaas, Lisa (2000). "Minorities Are Crossing The Digital Divide," *PC Week*, January 31, 65–69.

# Chapter 5

# The Marginalization Process

In the previous chapter we concluded that the digital divide begins at home and, if not corrected, it spreads around the world. Indeed the digital divide in the United States has not been corrected and it is spreading. The speed of the spreading digital divide in this world is the key concern.

According to some estimates today, 80 percent of the world's population lives in countries that generate only 20 percent of the world's income. At the turn of the 20th century, the average family in the United States was nine times richer than the average family in Ethiopia. Today it is 60 times richer (Birdsall 1998). But we cannot entirely blame globalization and the digital divide for this worsening picture. There always have been haves and have-nots, but today we are experiencing the emergence of have-mores and have-nothings. This second part is more readily attributable to globalization and the digital divide.

Perhaps it is ironic that inequality is growing at a time when the victory of democracy and open markets over communism and closed markets is being celebrated. Both democracy and open-market developments seem to have the opposite effect from what is expected and what textbooks write about (Birdsall 1998).

As we add the Internet or the digital divide into this picture, claims that the Internet is inherently democratizing the world slowly but surely turn out to be incorrect (Shapiro 1999). In fact, it is contributing to the digital divide in a very noticeable manner. The following quote from Bacon (2000, p. 18) describes the picture:

Over 160,000 people, mostly women, work in Malaysia's big electronics plants—a production work force the size of the Silicon Valley's. The bosses are all foreign high-tech giants. Chips and circuit boards assembled on the line in Penang are shipped out to the U.S., Japan and Western Europe— the rich countries with markets.

If we reconsider the winner-takes-all concept, these 160,000 people are not receiving a handsome payment for their efforts. As was discussed in the previous chapter, Malaysia as a whole enjoyed a technology transfer. It may also have enjoyed the benefits of foreign direct investments, but this does not quite stop the marginalization process. Just as many less-developed countries participate in globalization and technology transfer, Malaysia has major problems as its workers attempt to empower themselves against the desires of the Western bosses and foreign high-tech giants who see that the workers are being marginalized. In other words, the workers do not share the benefits of the profitable trade transactions, they are not to be given higher wages, they cannot quite ask for better working conditions and the list of grievances goes on. It appears that the more benefits a few get, the worse off many become.

## MARGINALIZATION

Marginalization is considered as a guiding concept to evaluate diversity in knowledge development, as well as economic progress (Hall 1999). It is defined as "the peripheralization of individuals and groups from a dominant, central majority" (Hall 1999, p. 88).

Marginalization is about a lack of power, about not having access to economic benefits or information, not developing survival skills, not being able to be heard, not being able to express concerns, not being able to share experiences or learning that others have developed (Hall 1999). Marginalization, in other words, is being isolated from progress and being left alone to regress in a progressive world. Marginalization is modern-day slavery in a world that claims to be freer and more democratic than ever before.

## WHEN THE THIRD-WORLD COUNTRIES LOSE

There has been angst about global integration of markets that creates a further divide between well-educated workers (only a few) and their vulnerable, unskilled counterparts (large masses). The divide between the two has given more and more power to capital and has been forcing governments to unravel social safety nets (Birdsall 1998). These developments result in further maginalization of many countries and many groups within these countries.

According to Birdsall, technology is in the center of this drama of inequality, and this inequality is getting worse. First, movies, television and airplanes created further gaps between haves and have-nots and made them more visible. In the process, they also made the bitterness more noticeable. The entrance of computers truly made some of the have-nots become have-nothings, and many of the haves, have-mores. New production processes are generated and strengthened by computers. The proper use of information technology makes it possible to buy the lowest cost supplies, function in the most profitable markets and enter and exit quickly in different businesses, markets and industries with very large profits, at the risk of marginalization of the local economies or groups.

## HOW GLOBALIZATION DOESN'T WORK

Good (1996, p. 853) states: "Growth in trade translates into jobs. Every time we sell one billion dollars of American products and services overseas, we support about 14,000 U.S. jobs. In recent years, export-related jobs have grown six times faster than total employment." High-tech products are one-fourth of all U.S. exports. Just what happens to the receiving countries of these products and services? Not only are many U.S. customers experiencing a growth in income inequality, but they are also experiencing strong marginalization. In fact, unless there are far-reaching agreements and regulations, digital technology may devastate low-income communities or countries (Shapiro 1999).

As trade barriers are eliminated, slowly but surely, globalization or global integration becomes more noticeable. In the center of this trend is information technology. All of these directly, indirectly and in a combined manner create and contribute to marginalization (See Exhibit 5–1). Exhibit 5–1 has a straightforward message: it shows

Exhibit 5-1
Globalization and Its Impact

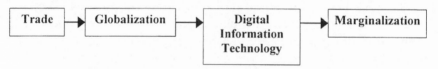

that trade leads to globalization and globalization, in conjunction with information technology, creates or contributes to marginalization.

Just how does this marginalization work? Exhibit 5–2 identifies the key causes of marginalization. There are eight scenarios presented in the exhibit. It must be realized that although each scenario can cause marginalization, many of these work simultaneously and interactively. And if they are working together in that fashion, they are creating a major negative synergy.

*Top-down foreign capital*: Perhaps unfortunately, foreign capital comes into the country from top to the top. In other words, the real benefits are enjoyed by the domestic industrialists who are at the top. The banks or major corporations receive the money. It is supposed to trickle down, but it is a very weak trickle down that hardly trickles. In the meantime, the country uses its resources ineffectively, damages its environment, and the gap between the rich and poor gets wider.

*Developing access to information*: A small fraction of populations in less-developed countries gains access to information through IT. Some of this information indicates opportunities as well as bargains. Those who develop access to information gain much power and become very rich, while the rest of the society stagnates or even gets worse.

*Gaining access to knowledge*: Globalization requires particular emphasis on speed, flexibility or versatility. Furthermore, it requires an understanding of the impact of permanent changes (Smadja 1999). Most of these requirements can be met by gaining access to knowledge. This is more specific and more productive than developing access to information. But if the society, in general, is not a learning society that puts much emphasis on generation of information, distribution of information and hence accumulating knowledge, globalization will cause those who have knowledge to move ahead at the expense of those who do not (Samli 2001). Those few who have

**Exhibit 5-2**
**Marginalization Process**

| Scenario | Outcome |
|---|---|
| 1) Top-down private foreign capital. | Profit motivation helps a few skilled workers and local partners discriminate against the rest. |
| 2) A few develop access to information through IT. | They gain much power and fortune while the rest of the society gets worse. |
| 3) Some of the IT users and a few others have access to knowledge. | They establish partnerships and joint ventures and a few get very rich while the rest of the society deteriorates. |
| 4) As information, capital and know-how flow, a powerful top-down management process emerges. | Gives much more power to the already powerful and widens the gap between the powerful and powerless. |
| 5) Using much more capital-intensive industries because of cost and efficiency reasons. | Unskilled labor loses more jobs, and employment rises. |
| 6) Domestic governments to protect their turf become overly protective. | The country goes back to the dark ages. |
| 7) The rich buy many unnecessary products and services from world markets. | The precious foreign exchange disappears. |
| 8) Private investments enter and become very profitable. | They take out of the country more than they brought in. |

enough knowledge and experience can partner with foreign firms and get very rich, while the rest of the society may deteriorate. Of course, it should not mean that while a few get extremely rich, the rest of the society must deteriorate. However, this is typical in the marginalization process. In the short run particularly, marginalization works in the form of a zero-sum game, which means the winner will win as losers lose. This is because of the limitation of the resources and gross domestic output. These countries' economies cannot be charged immediately.

*Top-down management processes*: Unless there is a bottom-up component, management processes, particularly in globalization, are mostly top-down. This process implies only a trickle-down effect, if any. All of the flows mentioned in chapter 1 give much more power to those in the country who already are powerful. This widens the gap between the powerful and the powerless by creating a marginalization activity. Even if it is not meant to be that way, this marginalization event may be the de facto impact of some groups' gaining extraordinary powers through globalization.

*Capital-intensiveness*: Most high-tech products are capital-intensive. In fact, most products in the product flow or international trade, which is a critical component of the globalization process, are high-tech and capital-intensive. As such, they favor capital. As production of capital-intensive products becomes widespread, the production of labor-intensive products or low-tech products becomes less important. Labor-intensive production activity uses unskilled labor. As the demand for these products lessens in favor of high-tech products, unskilled labor loses more jobs. As a few skilled workers benefit, unskilled workers get marginalized. There are many more unskilled workers than skilled workers in countries that are being marginalized.

*Domestic protectionism*: Although free flow of capital, know-how, information and labor imply more successful globalization, this does not mean the withdrawal of government from the economy (Rosen 2000). Indeed, the government must first establish an institutional framework for the market to function effectively. Second, it must develop the infrastructure for efficient economic input/output activity that will encourage the private sector. As one government attempts to accomplish these two very major functions, the country's economy may become or may appear to be less open and more overtly protectionist. Some authors maintain that such protectionism may cause serious marginalization itself (Ng and Yeats 1997). If the domestic government cannot provide opportunities for free trade or direct foreign investments, then the country may further regress in a progressive world. But, as will be seen in chapters 12 and 13, domestic protectionism under specific circumstances can also be quite useful.

*Unnecessary consumption*: Many consumers all over the world can buy many products and better satisfy their needs, even needs they may not have had before. For a rich country such as the United States, which has a hard currency that can be exchanged or accepted anywhere, this is not a problem. In fact, by purchasing certain imported products very cheaply, Americans can save money and buy products or services that are more important, such as computers or education. However, in less-developed countries, there is always a critical shortage of foreign hard currency, which must be used for critical industrial and high-tech products that are needed for the country's development. If the country's foreign exchange supply is used for expensive and unnecessary luxury products that are not valuable from an economic development perspective, then the rest of the country is marginalized.

*Payments for foreign investments*: Direct foreign investments enter the country rather swiftly. They generate much profit, but after all is said and done, these profits also are taken out of the country rather swiftly. If the investments do not create an economic ripple effect in that they generate important domestic growth, the profits and interests that are taken out of the country will outstrip the benefits of these FDIs. As a result, the less-developed country's economy is partially, or fully, marginalized.

As seen in Exhibit 5–2 and discussed above, globalization is not a panacea, it is not a cure and it is not even a simple remedy. Although in some cases it is wonderful, in most cases it has a destabilizing and even a debilitating effect. Two experiences are particularly significant, Russia and the African continent.

## THE RUSSIAN EXPERIENCE

Perhaps one of the most critical problems of globalization is that it can come into the country like a shock. Coming out of communism and having had no experience in capitalism, globalization has been a shock to a very fragile Russian economy. About 15 percent of Russians who have access to capital, information and trade—including the Mafia, as well as the church—have become extremely successful and rich. At the writing of this book, rumors are that about 85 percent of Russians are even worse off now than they were during the communist era, which was not a point in Russian history to brag about. Marginalization of the Russian society is so strong that prospects for progress are almost nonexistent. Illegal transactions such as white slavery, selling weapons to questionable parties and smuggling unauthorized products and services in and out of the country are all ongoing counterproductive events.

## THE AFRICAN EXPERIENCE

Although Africa participated in major export activity in the early 1960s, its share in world trade did not remain the same or increase proportionately as world trade increased in volume and as globalization accelerated. This is attributed to overprotectionist government policies. Such protectionism interfered with African trade and marginalized parts of the participating countries (Ng and Yeats 1997). Although this explanation is rather common, it is also rather simplistic. The present author maintains that in Africa, as well as in Russia, the political stability (or lack thereof) played a critical role. This point is further discussed in chapter 12. However, suffice it to say that a country's economy cannot make progress in the midst of political chaos.

## WHY THE FOUR TIGERS?

After having briefly observed the Russian and African experiences, one can ask the serious question: Why were the Four Tigers so successful under the same prevailing globalization and trade issues? This question is related to a very important issue. If the less-developed countries knew the answer, globalization would be much more successful, and perhaps marginalization could be eliminated.

Hong Kong, Singapore, Taiwan and South Korea are called the Four Tigers for their extraordinary economic performance in the 1970s, 1980s and early 1990s. It must be emphasized here that these Four Tigers do not have any extraordinary natural resources. In general, they focused on labor-intensive industries in the 1960s and then shifted the direction of their industrial development to focusing more on capital-intensive and particularly skilled labor-intensive economic sectors (Kotler, Jatusripitak and Maesincee 1997). Singapore, for example, had an increase in its GDP per capita from $950 in 1970 to $12,300 at the beginning of the 1990s. The other Tigers' performances have been equally impressive.

Why has marginalization not been experienced in this part of Asia?

Conventional wisdom in conservative economies is that these countries concentrated on free trade. But this author believes that this is a necessary, but not a sufficient condition. Kotler, Jatusripitak and Maesincee (1997) put forth three key success factors displaying conditions that they maintain are not likely to be duplicated:

1. The ideologies of elites in these countries and growth-oriented policies of the government were congruent.
2. Even though all elites were not included in economic development, they were included in the wealth-sharing programs. They benefited from these programs and hence did not create a counterproductive schism or divisiveness.
3. Honest and competent bureaucracies and economists were left alone and kept free of unnecessary political pressures.

Obviously three further observations emerge. It is critical to realize that there were elites, there were very active and unopposed governments and there were no political disorders. These are extremely critical observations. They are discussed in Chapters 8 and 9.

## THE POWERS OF FREE TRADE

Trade is a necessary but not a sufficient condition for economic development and globalization without marginalization. Thus, free trade has power and plays a critical role. It may not be a sufficient condition, but without free trade, globalization and its benefits cannot materialize.

Therefore, it is not trade itself that is being questioned, but rather its aftermath. Once trade takes place, resultant globalization is what is needed to be concentrated on. The impact of this resultant globalization is not necessarily even or fair. Those who trade benefit, but these benefits do not penetrate the rest of society. So they are not evenly distributed. That creates even worsening conditions in already questionable economic conditions.

## FREE BUT NOT FAIR

Free trade describes an accelerated growth in global investments because of dynamic technologies, improved communication and transportation systems. It simultaneously stands for the rising demand for new consumer products and the high cost of labor in developed countries. Finally it refers to the explosive increase in the number of companies investing globally (O'Donovan 1999). But if in the process some people, particularly women and indigenous minorities, are marginalized, this free trade and concomitant globalization is not fair. It has been said that free trade without fairness would not last (O'Donovan 1999). What is fairness? How long will it last? How can it be made fair? Can something be done for prevention? These are very critical questions. Some of them will be addressed in chapters 12 and 13. Just who can compete in the global arena is perhaps the most critical question.

## WHO CAN COMPETE?

Foreign direct investments, technology transfer, partnership and other aspects of globalization do not imply that all countries can make enough progress and become active as well as gainful participants in globalization. Some countries are so marginalized that they may never have the gainful participant status. It is unique and impressive that the Four Tigers have managed so well. But all less-developed countries do not have such determination, discipline and a strong, benevolent government. The outside free traders do not care about the well-being of the country. They are more concerned about trade and profits. In addition to the fact that all countries cannot be like the Four Tigers, purely trade-based economic development can be very volatile. While the country stimulates its economic development through trade, inside the country the discrepancy between the have-mores and have-nothings grows to a point of no return.

## THE ASIAN CRISES

The Asian crises of 1997 and 1998 brings the debate over the nature of the globalization process, the relative role of nation-states and economic development into focus. Although there are specific reasons given and theories have been developed to explain this crisis, one thing is certain: globalization and extreme trade dependency can cause sudden and very deep shocks in the participating countries' economies. Furthermore, such externally created shocks are difficult to control or pacify domestically. Thus it is not only marginalization that globalization can cause. The Asian crises indicate that after a number of years of large-volume trading and large inflows of foreign investments, everything can suddenly come to a halt. At that point, the most globalized country can be the most vulnerable (Harsch 1999).

One aspect of marginalization that has not been discussed up to now is international business cycles. As Third World countries globalize, they become very dependent on international trade. Some industrialized countries, notably the United States, go through business cycles. Although they experience hardship, they manage to survive. However, Third World countries that are pulled into the globalization process are already being marginalized and feel these business cycles very strongly. They do not have the economic might or reserves to survive such a hardship. Hence they become devastated.

## SUMMARY

This chapter deals with the most important problem that is related to and perhaps caused by globalization. Globalization creates large numbers of isolated individuals and groups who do not have power, do not have information, do not develop skills, do not have a voice and do not share the experiences or learning of others. The marginalization process can take place in different forms and is caused by different forces. Eight marginalization scenarios are identified in the chapter: (1) top-down foreign capital, (2) developing access to information, (3) gaining access to knowledge, (4) top-down management process, (5) capital intensiveness, (6) domestic protectionism, (7) unnecessary consumption, and (8) payments for foreign investments.

Although in some circles globalization is shown as a panacea for economic poverty, at times it is not even a simple remedy. However, the Four Tigers, have done extremely well by it. Therefore, there are possibilities for superlative success. Over and beyond free trade, which is a necessary but not sufficient element, these countries have had something special. They have a powerful elite participating in the economy, they have had very proactive governments and they did not experience political disorder. Unlike the Four Tigers, Russia and most of Africa have been experiencing extreme cases of marginalization because of free trade. Free trade is the necessary ingredient of globalization. But "free" does not mean "fair." Free trade without fairness will not last long, but can cause damage that may last a long time.

Finally, the Asian financial crises of 1997 and 1998 showed that globalization has other major negative impacts besides marginalization. The countries that tie themselves and their well-being almost exclusively to world trade can become very vulnerable. If, for some reason, there is some disruption in the world's capital flow or product and services flow, these countries can face a chaotic financial and economic dilemma.

## REFERENCES

Bacon, David (2000). "Globalization's Two Faces, Both Ugly," *Dollars and Sense*, March, 18–24.

Birdsall, Nancy (1998). "Life Is Unfair: Inequality in the World," *Foreign Policy*, Summer, 76–94.

Fujita, Kunika (2000). "Asian Crises, Financial Systems and Urban Developments," *Urban Studies*, November, 2197–2218.

Good, Mary Lowe (1999). "Technology and Trade," *Law and Policy in International Business*, Summer, 853–864.

Hall, Joanne M. (1999). "Marginalization Revisited: Critical, Postmodern and Liberation Perspectives," *Advances in Nursing Science*, December, 88–102.

Harsch, Ernest (1999). "Africa, Asia and Anxieties About Globalization," *Review of Political Economy*, March, 117–123.

Kotler, Philip, Jatusripitak, Somkid and Maesincee, Suvit (1997). *The Marketing of Nations*. New York: The Free Press.

Ng, Francis and Yeats, Alexander (1997). "Open Economies Work Better! Did Africa's Protectionist Policies Cause Its Marginalization in World Trade?" *World Development*, No. 6, 889–904.

O'Donovan, Leo T. (1999). "A Dialogue in Hope: Reflections on Ethical Issues in a Globalizing Economy," *Americas*, September 11, 6, 18.

Rosen, George (2000). "Globalization, Growth and Marginalization," *Pacific Affairs*, Winter, 572.

Samli, A. Coskun (2001), *Empowering the American Consumer*. Westport, CT: Quorum Books.

Shapiro, Andrew L. (1999). "The Internet," *Foreign Policy*, Summer, 14–22.

Smadja, Claude (1999). "Living Dangerously: We Need New International Mechanisms to Harness Globalization's Potential to Generate Prosperity," *Time*, February 22, 94.

# Chapter 6

# Miracles Do Not Happen So Easily

One of the most important aspects of globalization is that certain products, certain brands and certain company names become extremely well-known. Everyone in the world knows IBM, Xerox or Mercedes Benz, for example. All the young people around the world like to wear Ralph Lauren Polo or Tommy Hilfiger attire. They certainly recognize Nike or Reebok. In fact, one can find the well-recognized Nike swoosh logo everywhere. Through globalization and, of course, through very powerful marketing, international brand equities are established. These powerful brands generate very large profits. Any highly profitable brand encourages the emergence of imitations.

## DEMONSTRATION EFFECT THEN AND NOW

In the late 1950s, in graduate economics classes, a concept called "demonstration effect" used to be discussed. The theory posited that less-developed countries typically are impressed with the more luxurious lifestyles that exist in developed countries. Hence they will try to imitate such lifestyles and waste their savings and resources. As a result, they will not be able to develop their domestic economies.

Of course, in those days the demonstration effect would be triggered only by movies, traveling and travelogues. Today, if there were to be such a demonstration effect, it would easily be triggered by global television, the Internet and other communication media, including international magazines, books and online communication alternatives. On the basis of classical economic theory, one might say that the demonstration effect is not only alive and well, but rather it is gaining momentum as globalization accelerates. However, could it be possible that this demonstration effect could also have positive implications? Or, at least, could it be a stimulant that might play a different and more important role in less-developed economies?

The well-recognized products, brands and companies just mentioned can easily whet the appetite of people in those countries. If people cannot buy the originals, they can buy imitations. Such an orientation has led to the emergence of two important concepts: international product piracy, and international industrial espionage.

## INTERNATIONAL PRODUCT PIRACY

Because of the intensified global communications process, more and more products, brands and makers are recognized and desired. Being part of the "in-group" or considering oneself "arrived" creates a very strong desire for the possession of products with these brand identifications.

In the underground bazaars of Istanbul, one can find Ralph Lauren and Tommy Hilfiger apparel at reasonable prices. Although the quality might not be as high as the originals, these domestically produced pirated products are not so bad. The most important aspect of this phenomenon is that these somewhat desirable and sophisticated products are being produced in that country. This is not only an indication of successful technology transfer, but also the opposite of what the demonstration effect originally maintained, in that if the desire for these products that is created by the demonstration effect stimulates industrial development, the demonstration effect functions in the positive direction. Is there not a possibility that because of the prevailing desire for some of these products, industrialists in these countries may go out of their way to get perhaps the "most appropriate technology" and subsequently the most "up-to-date technology"? This may break down the vicious cycle of economic underdevelopment that afflicts less-developed countries.

Breaking up the vicious cycle of economic underdevelopment here is based on four elements. First, the country experiences successfully transferred technology that may spill over to other industries. Second, it creates relatively better-paying jobs. Anytime a technology is successfully transferred, better-than-average-paying jobs are created. Third, by buying locally made products as a substitute for imports, the country uses its international buying ability for more important products or services. Fourth, perhaps some of these pirated products can be exported for costs much less than the originals. Turks may export their pirated Polo shirts to Iran, Russia or anywhere in the world.

For years there were rumors that factories in Hong Kong would produce regular apparel during the daytime and then produce pirated jeans and other products during the night. If these rumors are correct, obviously these activities have had a very positive impact on Hong Kong's economy.

Rumor has it that a Turkish manufacturer pirated the German model of a washer and dryer. The German company took the Turkish company to court and won the case. Subsequently, the Turkish executives received a call from the German company. The gist of the conversation was for each part just to forget about the court's judgment and for the two companies to merge. The Turkish product was as good as the German product, and the cost was much lower. Certainly such merger episodes would help both parties, but particularly the Turkish economy. But then it must be recognized that if such episodes repeat themselves in the Turkish economy, Turkey will become a better customer for many other consumer and industrial products coming from many countries. This is a critical economic development scenario that is like expecting a miracle, which is rather costly. But if it is successful, the benefits to all involved are great.

Economic development is not exactly the motivation for piracy. In other words, companies in the Third World do not pirate to develop their economies. They simply try to make money by imitating well-known products. There are more readily available temptations and motivations that lead to international product piracy other than developing the country's economy. However, micromanagement such as product piracy may have significant macroeconomic implications such as the economy's development. There are at least six factors or forces that stimulate and/or encourage international piracy: (1) availability of information, (2) not having resources for research, (3) needing quick results, (4) attitude toward intellectual capital, (5) not having a research and development background and (6) not having a legal structure. These are illustrated in Exhibit 6–1.

*Availability of information*: As globalization accelerates, availability and accessibility of information are increasing disproportionately. Information about the product, production methods, alternative procedures to improve the product or lower production costs are all very available. Acquiring the equipment to produce the product is also rather easy. If an unknown manufacturer has access to all this information, it is not likely to start its own brand and product line. The manufacturer will most likely pirate an already existing well-known product.

*Not having resources for research*: Any kind of research is expensive. Product research that is conducted in the United States is perhaps more expensive than many other types of research and more expensive than research done in other countries. Developing a product from scratch calls for lots of time and many effort-consuming steps. From conceptualization of a new product until it is introduced to the market, the steps involved in the new product development curve—such as concept testing, product specification that identifies the product's key features and prototype development—are all important and costly steps. Many countries do not have enough resources to go through such a costly process.

*Needing quick results*: Many businesses around the world, particularly many in less-developed countries, feel the pressure to respond quickly to changing market conditions. Others feel that they have to move fast to take advantage of some existing, quite likely temporary, opportunities. Under these circumstances, product piracy becomes a natural outcome. I have had many personal experiences in this area. In one case while I was interviewing the director of medium-sized textile factory, an engineer entered the office with a sample of material that he had just pirated from pictures he had seen in a fashion magazine. The director was elated.

*Attitude toward intellectual capital*: Particularly in Eastern cultures, an invention, new knowledge, a new book and so on are to be shared. These are not considered private property as much as they are in the West. They are considered community property. This is one easy explanation of how one American CD multiplies into a million copies or more in China.

*Not having a research and development background*: Not only do

**Exhibit 6-1**
**Factors Behind Product Piracy**

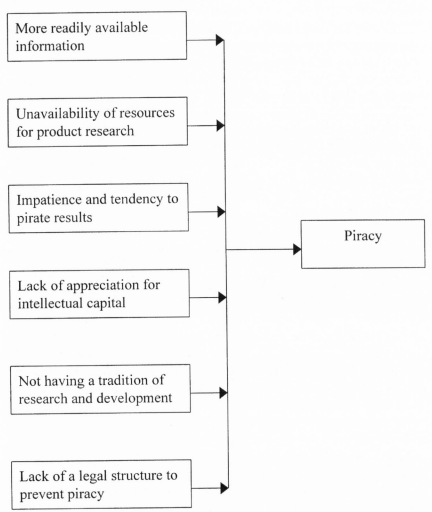

some countries and companies not have the resources for research, they also lack a research and development tradition. They are impressed when there is a new innovation or an idea in the West, but they do not think in terms of developing something better. Instead they imitate or pirate. Even Japan has been accused time and again of being more of an imitator than a creator. It is almost too bad that many of these countries do not have a research and development tradition. Each country and each culture being different and unique, there could be many new ideas and innovations that could make the world a better place and its inhabitants a lot happier.

*Not having a legal structure*: Finally, not having a worldwide legal structure to police illegal activities, such as piracy, provides encouragement for those activities. Not only is it difficult for other countries to follow and abide by the Western value system of private ownership and intellectual property rights, it is extremely time-consuming and costly. There have been numerous attempts to explain the importance of enforcing intellectual property rights, and then to establish an international system to enforce these rights (Arbetter 1994).

In the meantime, simple estimates of the cost of global piracy to American businesses run from $100 billion to $200 billion a year. However, these piracy acts may be stimulating certain national economies that are not likely to be stimulated otherwise. This is a costly proposition, but in the absence of a global legal authority, much of the time lawsuits are very costly and extremely time-consuming. It is almost impossible to have quick decisions from the courts in cases where piracy may be the issue. In fact, in some countries it has been claimed that government officials support piracy. If indeed this rumor is factual, it becomes even more difficult to establish a worldwide legal order to deal with the piracy of intellectual property. This is a costly issue, particularly for the American business sector. However, in the absence of a global authority, companies can be instructed to take any of numerous counterpiracy measures as a long-term solution (Samli, Jacobs and Jedlik 2001). Over and beyond this, part of the piracy, strangely enough, is almost like economic aid to these countries. In fact, such micropractices could have far-reaching macroeconomic implications that are very desirable. The U.S. government could help the companies that are hurt by piracy practices and consider part of the total losses as an economic aid program. It must always be kept in mind that economic progress for have-nots, which will prevent them from becoming have-nothings, is a very good move for the industrial world. If these countries improve their economies, they will become better markets for American-made goods and services.

International product piracy is complicated and costly for American businesses. However, it is not quite as complicated and expensive as international industrial espionage, which may have the opposite implications of product piracy practices.

## INTERNATIONAL INDUSTRIAL ESPIONAGE

In addition to all the factors leading to piracy presented in Exhibit 6–1, industrial espionage has additional factors stimulating such activity. It is important to distinguish espionage from piracy. In piracy, a product (mostly a consumer product) is imitated with the intent of selling it in place of the original. Thus it partially helps an import substitute or an exportable item. Espionage, on the other hand, deals with highly technical, secretive and expensive products and processes. It would take some major activity to steal or imitate these products, but the unscrupulous national leaders of our times are very tempted to steal these formulas or products to enhance their evil goals. These may be complicated and expensive industrial products, very sophisticated military equipment or the most recent computer- and software-related innovations, among others. The additional motivating activity factors, over and beyond those shown in Exhibit 6–1, are lack of protection and increasing value of trade secrets.

*Lack of protection*: Most American firms do not have specific programs for protecting their vital secrets (Duffy 1999). A company's basic research, product development, pricing and marketing plans are all targets of global industrial espionage. Basic research findings and product development plans are critically valuable for spies from different countries, but particularly less-developed countries, since they do not have research capabilities.

*Increasing value of trade secrets*: Global industrial espionage activity is accelerating because of the increasing value of trade secrets. Major American companies such as IBM, Kodak, 3M and AT&T have been and are targets of espionage activity (Barth 1998). This is primarily because their trade secrets lead to very profitable ventures.

Global industrial espionage is estimated to cost American businesses about $300 billion per year. Certainly no one can condone such costly illegal activity. The U.S. counterintelligence community has specifically identified the suspicious collection and acquisition activities of foreign agencies from at least 23 countries. Of these, 12 particularly emphasize trade-secret information (National Counter Intelligence Center 1997). It is important, however, to think of the fact that global industrial espionage can be at least partially considered as successful technology transfer. There are numerous methods of spying. However, some of these almost by definition will stimulate the spies' home economy. As in the previous section regarding piracy,

Exhibit 6-2
**Different Espionage Techniques and Their Economic Impact on Spy Countries**

**Economic Benefits to Spy Country**

|                                        | High | Low |
|----------------------------------------|------|-----|
| **High** | Reversed Engineering<br>Early Product Announcements | Business Intelligence<br>Dumpster Diving |
| **Personal or Corporate Gains to Spies**<br><br>**Low** | Elicitation<br>Electronic Interception | Lawsuits<br>Insider Treason<br>Industrial Theft |

but even more seriously, it can be argued that some good could come out of industrial espionage as well.

Exhibit 6–2 illustrates some of the most common espionage techniques. Some of these are classified as economically beneficial, as well as providing corporate gains to spies and their respective companies simultaneously. But others are very questionable. The upper left quadrant of the exhibit illustrates two such techniques. The first is a common and rather involved procedure called reversed engineering. As an American company introduces an advanced model of a portable air conditioning unit, manufacturers in Egypt, for instance, take the unit apart and then put it back together to see how it was made. Whereas it may have taken a long time and some significant research expenditures to develop this product, Egyptians can learn how to produce it very quickly by reversed engineering. If such an activity can stimulate the development of a new industry, or at least provide parts and components to international importers, the marginalization process through globalization can be stopped and counteracted. Similarly, announcements from the American company bragging about the specifics of forthcoming models or a new product line can give much new information that pirates can benefit from and can help them develop similar products.

The lower left quadrant mentions elicitation. This refers to attending scientific seminars and trade shows, along with unsolicited telephone calls. Such techniques are also important in obtaining bits of information about new developments. In such cases, however, the spies are less likely to be equipped with the engineering skills that are likely in reversed engineering. This can be beneficial to the society. Elicitation and electronic interception would be more involved in starting industries and, if that happens, it is beneficial to the country's economy. However, spying in this manner may mean that the spies are less likely to benefit if they do not already have production facilities.

In the upper right quadrant, business intelligence and dumpster diving are listed. In business intelligence, spies may get business secrets illegally or legally. But simply acquiring business secrets does not do much for the country's economy. Dumpster diving means obtaining waste papers, shredded documents, and the like. This approach may help the spy advance his status in the company, but does not do much for the economy.

The lower right quadrant indicates some of the spying techniques that do not do much for the Third World economy or even personal advancement of the spy. Lawsuits in the United States and some European countries give much information about a company, its products and its operations. Trying to get employees to spy is common in the West, but a less-developed country may not be successful in this. Similarly, industrial theft is not a normal activity for less-developed countries. Even though, at times, France, Japan and China, among others, have been accused of being engaged in such an activity, it has been maintained that some of the less-developed countries are also getting involved.

## THE FAIRNESS ISSUE

The fairness, or lack thereof, of piracy and espionage is partially related to the culture and partially to the political system. The cultural aspect of fairness is related to possession. Thus, unlike in many Western cultures, in Eastern cultures intellectual property is considered to be community property and something that needs to be shared with others in the society.

The political aspect of fairness in this case goes back to legal ownership. In the capitalist system, ownership is legalized and intellectual property, just as any other property, is also legalized. Certainly, from the Western capitalistic point of view, piracy and espionage appear to be unfair and are declared illegal. But in the absence of a legal structure that acts swiftly and is accepted by all parties, the legality or illegality of piracy and espionage become moot issues. Within the constraints of a country, like the United States or Germany, which have swift and effective recourse against these illegal activities, what could one do legally against the pirates if, say, the judges or other government officials were part of the spying organizations? This is claimed to be the case in some countries.

This is not condoning piracy and espionage, but is tackling the problem individually. Companies are mostly on their own in attempting to counteract or totally stop piracy and espionage. Many major American companies have been paying a fortune to counterintelligence companies to be protected against piracy. However, this costly proposition is not foolproof.

If left alone and if they have to solve the problem themselves, what would American and West European companies do to protect against piracy and espionage? Certainly, some counterintelligence effort is necessary, but how much? If the counterespionage effort becomes prohibitively expensive, then the firm may have to be engaged in a major offensive strategy. This means that instead of putting money into espionage prevention, the firm puts more money into research and development (R&D). If the additional R&D activity is likely to yield a significant competitive advantage through product improvement and marketing, then proactive firms are likely to take this position. This way, as spies develop imitations, the company that generated the original product will be ahead by a more advanced version of it, which is created by additional R&D. In a sense, this will stimulate international competition through R&D, which is beneficial to the world community. It must be reiterated that this is still a very special case and does not distort the typical flow of technology which is still from developed to developing countries.

Emphasizing R&D does not preclude taking precautionary measures. All companies can implement some basic activities that are not costly and would eliminate obvious piracy attempts (Shanley and Crabb 1998). These activities, among others, include: removing all computers, printers and fax machines from common work areas and R&D sites; developing password-protected screen savers for all computer terminals; and not allowing company retirees to have access to company secrets. By implementing these precautionary measures, the bulk of the possible espionage activity can be prevented, and then the firm can put major portions of its assets into R&D. Thus, the fear of espionage can keep companies ahead of spies. By the same token, those successful spies may develop replicas of the older models as they

establish industries in their countries, which would reduce the marginalization effects of globalization.

Thus, at least partially, piracy and espionage are stimulants for
global competition; they are perhaps more genuine development factors in less-developed countries. Piracy and espionage in themselves
are also some versions of technology transfer that are not desirable
to senders (developed countries), but are the most welcomed activity
by the receivers (less-developed countries).

## WHAT ARE THE PARAMETERS?

To a certain extent both piracy and espionage have some benefits
to pirates and spies. But if there are no redeeming features of the
counterfeited product, or if they endanger the lives of the innocent
users, then that is a different situation.

At the time of writing this book, this author has been exposed to
many bits of information relating to a "global epidemic of counterfeit
medicines" (*Business Week*, 2001). Some of these are dangerous to
the health and well-being of the users and, therefore, this type of
counterfeiting activity must be very closely scrutinized by the global
community. The difference between illegal and dangerous products,
and a genuine attempt to develop a good product, is like day and
night. Exhibit 6–3 illustrates five different counterfeit activities where
the outcome is not likely to make a contribution to the counterfeiter's
economy and can harm large numbers of people who are not informed or properly protected. For instance, counterfeit AIDS medicine, if good, can be extremely useful. But if such medicine is not a
good imitation or a total fake, it can cause immeasurable damage.

One last aspect of piracy and espionage is what I call the "ripple
effect." Once technology is received, legally or illegally, the additional
knowledge can be used in other industries. Hence, knowledge and
experience can be applied to other industries. As a result, product
piracy, if it is successful, can generate information and experience that
will be used some similar and some not-so-similar industries.

## SUMMARY

There is an unusual message in this chapter that needs to be carefully understood. Although product piracy and industrial espionage
are very costly propositions for many Western countries and compa-

**Exhibit 6-3**
**Varieties of Counterfeit Medicine**

| Varieties | Description |
| --- | --- |
| Identical Copies | These are acceptable imitations |
| Look-A-Likes | The packaging and appearance may be accurate, but they do not have active ingredients and can be harmful |
| Rejects | Medications that are rejected by manufacturers are recycled in the black market |
| Relabeled | Authentic, but expired drugs are relabeled with later expiration date |
| Local Substitutes | Local imitation of some rare and expensive medications that could be good or bad |

*Source:* Adapted and revised from *Business Week* (2001).

nies, there are also some possible benefits. Globalization, by defini-tion, enhances the possibility of imitation and espionage. By the same token, it is globalization that makes piracy and espionage possible.

There are many reasons for less-developed countries or companies to be engaged in piracy or espionage. The chapter identified six such reasons: (1) availability of information, (2) unavailability of resources for research, (3) lack of time and need for fast results, (4) lack of respect for intellectual capital, (5) not having a tradition for R&D and (6) lack of a global legal structure.

As companies and countries are engaged in product piracy and in-dustrial espionage, they may develop their skills and respective in-dustries. Because of their positive motivation, these attempts are likely to become more successful than standard technology transfers.

By the same token, the countries and companies whose products or services are pirated or spied on are likely to put more effort and resources into R&D, so they can keep ahead of pirates and spies. This is a type of competition that will keep these countries and companies competitive and proactive. However, some types of piracy or espionage are not acceptable. They should never endanger lives and there should be a global general agreement to prevent such acts.

## REFERENCES

Arbetter, Lisa (1994). "Intelligence Policy in a Changing World," *Security Management*, May, 39–42.

Barth, Steve (1998). "Spy Vs. Spy," *World Trade*, August, 34–37.

*Business Week* (2001). "What Is in That Pill?" June 18, 60.

Duffy, B. (1999). "Espionage by Keystroke?" *U.S. News and World Report*, May 10, 18, 24.

National Counter Intelligence Center (1997). "1997 Annual Report to Congress on Foreign Economic Collection and Industrial Espionage," Annual Report to Congress, September, 1–16.

Samli, A. Coskun, Jacobs, Lawrence and Jedlik, Thomas (2001). "The Nightmare of International Product Piracy," *Industrial Marketing Management*, Fall, 499–509.

Shanley, Agnes and Crabb, Charlene (1998). "Corporate Espionage: No Longer a Hidden Threat," *Chemical Engineering*, December, 82–96.

# Chapter 7

# The More You Borrow

In Chapter 1, four flows were identified as accelerating forces behind globalization. Capital flow is particularly powerful in that process. As discussed in Chapter 1, free flow of funds has been an important boon to globalization and, as such, it has also impacted the marginalization process. After a detailed market analysis, *Business Week* (January 2001) has concluded that because of the rather free flow of capital, there have been many reckless investments that have done much harm.

It is admirable that both the International Monetary Fund (IMF or the Fund) and the World Bank (the Bank) are seriously concerned about poverty reduction throughout the world. In fact, the World Bank headquarters has built into its lobby wall the slogan, "Our dream is a world free of poverty," which is truly a dream (Easterly 2000). However, it is only a dream and, as such, it does not have much relationship to reality. Being concerned about poverty and knowing what to do about it are two separate issues. The globalization movement is, as Thomas Friedman (2000) called it, "Darwinism on Steroids," and it appears that the IMF and the World Bank are not doing anything about it except accelerating this process further. When the profit motive starts running throughout the world unchecked, concern about poverty is transferred to the back burner. These two organizations live in their own dogma-driven world.

Both the Bank and the Fund make many loans that are based on extremely indoctrinated and dogmatic macroeconomic and structural conditions which are put together in the manner of one-size-fits-all. In fact, they might have caused more harm than all of the wars of the 20th century put together. Their macroeconomic conditions include reducing the receiving countries' budget deficits, devaluating their currency and reducing domestic credit expansion. These conditions are somewhat reasonable although a special case can be made against each. But their structural conditions are particularly restrictive and rigid. They are not based on reality; they are based on extreme right-wing political beliefs. They include freeing controlled prices and interest rates, reducing trade barriers and privatizing state enterprises.

## QUESTIONABLE PRACTICES OF THE BANK AND THE FUND

Both the IMF and the Bank impose upon the prospective recipients of credit very rigid conditions that almost by definition benefit the creditors (the Fund and the Bank) and the rich financiers in the receiving country. The conditions imposed upon the prospective borrowers are classified into two categories: functional and structural.

### Functional Conditions

Three conditions are particularly emphasized: budget deficits, devaluation and credit limitation. There is a very rich literature illustrating how, under special circumstances, budget deficits make a positive contribution to the economy. Indeed, early on, this author did such studies and came up with some noteworthy conclusions that both the World Bank and the IMF would not possibly accept. If budget deficits are kept at reasonable levels and the excess funds of the country's currency are used for major economic improvement projects, in the long run they pay off well (Samli 1967).

Similarly, devaluation is an export-oriented activity for the crediting country. If the credit-receiving country does not have enough export potential and if it has to import some critical technologies such as energy, arms or information systems, devaluation by definition brings more money to the countries that are exporting these technologies to the credit-receiving country.

Reducing domestic credit expansion may not be a good measure if, for instance, credit expansion could have been used in beneficial areas of education, corporate-level productivity-increase-related activities and the like. Instead of such rigid rules, every case must be considered according to its merits. Every country has different needs that must be addressed carefully. There is no best way, but there are many good ways to accomplish economic growth. Countries should not be handcuffed up front so that they will be allowed to get credit.

## The Structural Conditions

Four structural conditions are particularly emphasized: freeing controlled prices, freeing interest rates, reducing trade barriers and privatizing state enterprises. These structural conditions create even more restrictive and rigid situations that may not benefit the receiving Third World country. Both the Bank and the Fund have their experiences from Western economies and believe their current sets of dogmas are all undisputed facts of life. The following illustrates:

Freeing controlled prices is a major dilemma. At the writing of this book, the State of California is having a major energy crisis. This is primarily attributable to ignorance and the indoctrination of the state decision-makers, who insisted on the privatization of the energy supply and in this way freed the controlled prices. All older textbooks about economics talk about oligopolies, which mean a few competitors controlling the market, and natural monopolies, which mean that having two of the same thing will be dysfunctional in our society. For instance, two competing railroads or two sets of highways are unnecessary and extremely costly; therefore, natural monopolies need to be regulated. Freeing the controlled prices in small and less-developed economies means letting monopolies or oligopolies function freely. Without controls, as in California, consumer price gouging becomes a practice. Uncontrolled oligopolies or monopolies take advantage of the consumer and make a very few people extremely rich.

Similarly, freeing interest rates in these countries gives unfair powers to banks and other lending institutions in terms of being able to discriminate against the relatively worse-off consumers who do not have much bargaining power as do the rich. If the interest rates are freely manipulated, then the banks can show reason for high risk and raise prices for their customers who have limited means. The end result of this activity is widening the gap between the rich and the poor in that country, causing more marginalization.

Reducing trade barriers is another structural condition that the Bank and the Fund insist on. Whereas elimination of trade barriers can be considered a boon for globalization and an increasing volume of global trade, it also allows some expensive and unnecessary imports of consumer nondurable goods such as chewing gum, Coca-Cola or some breakfast cereals. McDonald's in Moscow is a very popular eating place. It is also expensive by Russian standards and takes out much valuable and needed foreign currency. The fact is that in less-developed countries, importing these products dissipates hard currency supplies. While the country needs capital equipment for economic growth that is necessary to absorb the unemployed or the underemployed poor, spending resources on immediate consumption products creates a worsening situation for the poor.

Finally, privatization of state enterprises is one of the key conditions required of prospective borrowers. A number of issues can be raised about this particular point. First, in an economically less-developed country, there may not be enough private capital or know-how to start the necessary enterprises for economic growth. In such cases, it is necessary for the government to step in and initiate the project; otherwise, it will never get done. Second, in some cultures, working for the government attracts better talent than private business. In these societies, it is considered to be more glorious to work for the government than for the private sector. Thus, in order to use the available talent effectively, governments develop state enterprises. Third, while certain information may not be available in the private sector, the public sector may readily have information which is needed for the development of enterprises that are, again, essential for that country's economy. Fourth, there may be certain gaps in the economy. These gaps may indicate critical needs, such as, say, a fertilizer industry. The private sector may not have the initiative or the inclination to undertake such a task. The state enterprise may be the only way to accomplish this. Finally, many activities related to infrastructure development, such as building roads, sewerage systems or bridges, are not necessarily profitable undertakings, and hence, the private sector may not be at all interested in engaging in these activities. The nation's needs for public facilities and infrastructure must be taken care of so that the private sector can flourish. State enterprise here becomes a necessity so that the private sector will get the necessary support. Once state enterprises make the conditions friendly for the private sector, then the private sector truly blooms.

Exhibit 7–1 summarizes the conditions that the Bank and the Fund set forth before a country can qualify for a loan. This type of rigid, dogmatic and one-size-fits-all positioning not only does not generate the vibrant economy that the borrowing country needs to have so that the borrowed money will have the best performance for the borrowing economy, but it may actually deter the development of the economy. The receiving country, because of its different needs and different cultural values, will have to make some adjustments that are not likely well-suited to its needs and capabilities. To make matters worse, heavily indebted poor countries (HIPC) are under serious pressure to pay back the loans. If the progress is not there and the programs are not successful, then the recipients seem to be doing worse than before.

## HIPC INITIATIVE

Both the IMF and the World Bank have designed a framework to provide special assistance to these countries that are not doing well. If HIPCs pursue the adjustments and reform progress suggested by the IMF and the World Bank, most of which are presented in the previous section, then they will receive special assistance (IMF 2001). This is tantamount to establishing financial imperialism in the name of global capitalism. If the countries go along with the conditions so that they will qualify for a loan, then they cannot make real progress.

The measures required to qualify for a loan are so restrictive that, early on, these kinds of practices were coined "Brutal Banking" (*Multinational Monitor*, 1990). It has been repeatedly stated that these types of adjustments simply do not work (*Multinational Monitor* 2000).

The upshot of this special assistance is that the initiative does not appear to be effective enough to make a dent in the poverty that exists in HIPCs. Some analysts maintain that it is IMF's insistence on allowing all the currencies to free float that created the devastating financial crash in South East Asia in late 1990s. After the elimination of the gold standard, basically the world's major currencies were sep-

**Exhibit 7-1**
**Unrealistic Requirements of IMF and World Bank**

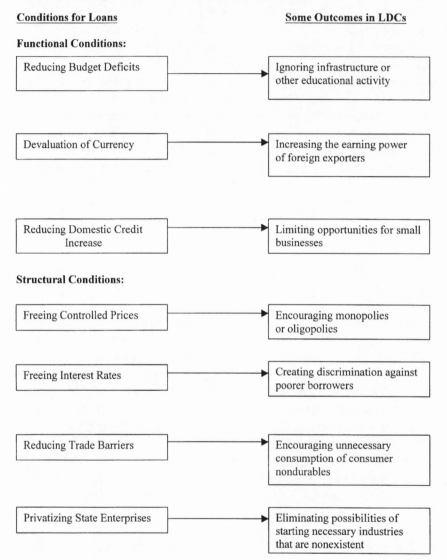

| Conditions for Loans | Some Outcomes in LDCs |
|---|---|
| **Functional Conditions:** | |
| Reducing Budget Deficits | Ignoring infrastructure or other educational activity |
| Devaluation of Currency | Increasing the earning power of foreign exporters |
| Reducing Domestic Credit Increase | Limiting opportunities for small businesses |
| **Structural Conditions:** | |
| Freeing Controlled Prices | Encouraging monopolies or oligopolies |
| Freeing Interest Rates | Creating discrimination against poorer borrowers |
| Reducing Trade Barriers | Encouraging unnecessary consumption of consumer nondurables |
| Privatizing State Enterprises | Eliminating possibilities of starting necessary industries that are nonexistent |

arated from gold and they gained or lost value in the world's markets based on demand and supply. However, many soft currencies of less-developed countries have pegged their currencies primarily on the dollar. As these currencies were disconnected from the hard currencies on which they were originally pegged, they took a very strong dive. They lost their value very fast and very sharply. This amounted to a major devaluation of these soft currencies. People in these countries lost their fortunes and credit, and money became scarce. Unemployment and business failures also became commonplace. As currencies devaluated, the impact on the poor was much more pronounced than on the rest of the economy (Hanke 2000). The IMF's insistence on these measures has been attributed to the indoctrinated and dogmatic political right wing in the United States and no longer has had much to do with the economic realities of these countries.

The Asian crises were repeated in Turkey in 2001 with similar types of devastation. The market system was not able to stabilize the free-floating Turkish lira. The small business sector simply disappeared because of the lack of money, credit and stability. Domestically, this event almost destroyed the country's small businesses. Similar experiences have taken place in numerous countries under the same circumstances. The Thai baht, for instance, crashed in 1997, as the government "was forced" to let baht float downward. The industrial sector of the country came to a halt (Friedman 2000).

These occurrences created tremendous setbacks for the Third World countries that are trying to become part of the globalization process. Getting away from political indoctrination and finding cures to this devastating situation is a very high priority for the lending organizations. There must be creative solutions before it is too late and all previously have-not countries become have-nothing countries.

## CREATIVE SOLUTIONS

The *extreme* capitalism, described thus far, that chooses dogma over practicality cannot generate creative solutions that are desperately needed. It has a very microorientation, and it is extremely lender-friendly.

Practicality is dependent on freedom from political dogma, an understanding of the country's problems and unique needs to solve the problems and, above all, flexibility in thinking. Unless such practicality is exercised, the marginalization process discussed earlier and particularly marginalization of the poor around the world will continue.

If lending organizations such as the IMF and World Bank could free themselves from political indoctrination and dogmatic ways of thinking, then they will be able to see that each country has different needs, priorities, capabilities and, hence, requires different and most assuredly appropriate solutions than permitted by the prevailing orientation of one-solution-fits-all.

It is extremely critical that a nation's administrators as well as its private sector are capable of developing constructive plans as to what kinds of undertakings would stimulate the country's economy. Understanding the country's economy and identifying as well as prioritizing different approaches that will benefit that economy the most as a whole will necessitate much more than what the IMF and World Bank require. In fact, what the Fund and the Bank require may not at all be in the best interest of the borrower nation's economy. It is critical to think about the recipient economy's growth.

## OUTSIDE FUNDING AND INSIDE GROWTH

Let us assume that the IMF and World Bank are charging a relatively low interest rate, say about 6 percent. It is critical to realize that this debt could be a pure and heavy burden on the borrowing economy. It must be understood that 6 percent interest in an inflation-and-overpopulation-laden economy may be totally impossible to handle. In other words, if the lenders charge an interest that is greater than the normal net economic growth of the borrower, then the whole proposition becomes useless. There is one exception. If the borrower has a specific plan so that the contribution of the borrowed money will yield a greater return in the domestic economy than what the lender is charging as interest, then the borrowing process makes sense. However, neither party can give assurance that such an outcome is very likely.

Exhibit 7–2 illustrates some of the less-developed countries' indebtedness. It is difficult to visualize how Liberia or Sudan can pay back those sums. As a result, domestic political unrest occurs, and the countries that are trying to pay back the loans find themselves under extraordinary pressures, due to excessive efforts to meet the guidelines. In such cases, the more these countries borrow, the deeper they sink. The principle is that the money that is loaned must do more good domestically than the interest charged. If the borrowed money cannot be put to good use so that it can generate more in-

**Exhibit 7-2**
**Indebtedness of Some LDCs**

| | |
|---|---|
| Afghanistan | $7,600,000 |
| Congo | 391,800,000 |
| Iraq | 55,000,000 |
| Liberia | 581,800,000 |
| Somalia | 251,600,000 |
| Sudan | 1,323,800,000 |

*Source:* Calculated from IMF Web page figures.

come than the interest charged, then it has no value. Outside funding without inside growth is a losing proposition.

It has been maintained by some analysts that the IMF and the World Bank interfere too much with the domestic politics of the borrowing countries. Furthermore, their policies do not generate prosperity or alleviate poverty. Therefore, it has been suggested that at least the IMF should be abolished (Hanke 2000). Just why is it that there is no economic progress in these countries?

## BARRIERS TO GROWTH

Those countries, companies or regions that are being marginalized have real difficulty overcoming a series of barriers and, in most cases, this failure is becoming more pronounced. Particularly, four specific areas are discussed here: outside competition, population explosion, lack of investments, and the vicious cycle.

*Outside competition*: If and when a country counts on globalization for its economic development, unless there are special skills, raw materials or natural endowments, it is very difficult for that country to compete with all the other countries competing for the same riches. As the globalization process progresses, competition to participate in the global market becomes keener. When the less-developed countries try to participate, they feel it is almost impossible to enter and make a mark that will translate into economic development.

In addition to trying to partake in the global trade, these countries have difficulty attracting foreign direct investments. They have difficulty borrowing as well. In all of these areas, competition is extremely keen. Much of the time, if direct foreign investments enter the country, they stay a very short time and quite often take out much more than invested originally. If the external help is limited, is there a possibility of growing internally? This topic is explored more completely in Chapter 8. However, it is necessary to reiterate that there are formidable barriers to growth domestically. Perhaps one of the major barriers to growth is population increase.

*Population explosion*: The old saying, "The rich get richer and the poor get more children," is unfortunately correct. When a country has a real growth rate (free of inflation in constant currency values) of 0 to 1 percent, but its population is increasing at a rate of 2 percent, on the average, everyone in that society becomes poorer. There are now more mouths to feed and more people with whom to share the wealth. But it does not stop here. Children are a major burden on society. Until they become productive citizens (if ever), they have to be taken care of. In societies where educational facilities or work opportunities are not present, it is natural for the young people to stay home longer and continue being a burden. Frederick Osborn (in Malthus, Huxley and Osborn 1960) made a statement that is worth repeating. He said, "The reduction of population or the rate of population growth is not an end in itself but only a means of advancing the more general objective of human welfare" (p. 117). Thus in many cases the population increase needs to be controlled so that the country can make economic progress. The People's Republic of China did not start making real progress in its economic growth until it established a one child per family policy. In the history of mankind, only China with such immense population—1.5 billion people—managed to grow its economy at a double-digit rate, more than 10 percent per year, which is powerful proof that a reasonable control of population increase is essential for economic growth. If population grows at a fast pace, the economy cannot afford to save and invest. Without savings and investments, the economy cannot grow.

*Lack of investments*: If outside competition does not allow the country's economy to grow and if the increasing population outstrips the economic growth, there will be no relief. There are not enough savings to invest for the future of the country. Under such circumstances the country may not even be standing still; it may be going backward. This is how have-nots become have-nothings. This whole situation is a vicious cycle (Samli 1985).

Very poor countries are typically entrapped in what this author calls *the vicious cycle.* It begins with the underdeveloped status of the economy, which implies low incomes. If incomes are low, then there will be low levels of savings. In economics it always has been stated that a low level of savings leads to a low level of investment. This is true because, technically, savings are equal to investments. A low level of investment creates a capital deficiency without which productivity remains low. As a result, the economy winds up at the same point as it started. Exhibit 7–3 illustrates this vicious cycle. If foreign investments do not come in, and domestic investments cannot be generated, then the vicious cycle continues. Certainly, foreign borrowing is a major alternative here. If the money that is borrowed from outside private and public sources can be used for economic development activity, then the results can be spectacular. However, as has been discussed earlier in this chapter, the lending organizations are more on the side of making money and protecting the riches of their own investors than worrying about the economic development activities in which the borrowers are engaged. In fact, it is unfortunately worth reiterating that the more some countries have borrowed, the worse shape they have gotten into.

In private life, at the consumer level, there is a general belief that people who do not need to borrow can borrow a lot of money; however, those who desperately need to borrow cannot. This statement is unfortunately true at the international level also. Those countries that need help desperately cannot get help to break the vicious cycle. Globalization, partly because it encourages the free flow of capital, makes it worse in the sense that the credits and/or investments coming from outside are more concerned with payoffs or paybacks than with the economic progress of the borrowers or recipients. Thus, unless the Third World country is very shrewd in the area of economic development and has an economic machine that is carefully put together, it does not have much of a chance. Unless the lenders or investors are capable of forgoing their present revenues, at least partially, or for a period of time, there is little hope of stopping or at least reducing the pace of the marginalization process.

Thomas Friedman (2000) talks about bad borrowing principles and

Exhibit 7-3
The Vicious Cycle of Economic Underdevelopment

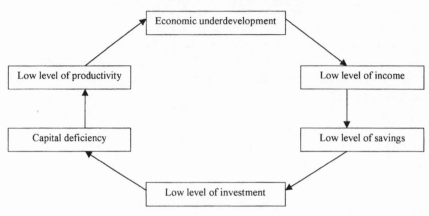

practices. However, he does not quite articulate the power of the lenders and their ability to create powerfully bad lending practices as described in this chapter. In other words, accusing the borrowers of bad borrowing practices will do nothing for the global poor. It is much more critical for the lenders to make sure that being a creditor in this case is not understood to be just making money for a few financiers. Giving credit to countries must generate greater economic benefit to the borrower than to the creditor. This does not mean that the creditor will not make money. It simply means that the borrower's benefits and progress are put on the front burner in the complex schemes of finance. It must be further articulated that if the borrower's economy improves, the borrower becomes a better customer for all that globalization offers, including borrowing more.

## SUMMARY

The main theme of this chapter is: If you are a Third World country, the more you borrow, the deeper you sink. It is maintained here that the International Monetary Fund and the World Bank, knowingly or unknowingly, are not truly friends of the have-nots. Their first interest is in protecting the monies that rich donors or investors have given.

There are many strings attached to the loans that are borrowed by Third World countries. The lending organizations have both functional and structural requirements for the borrowing countries. Functionally, they insist on reducing budget deficits. Also they insist on devaluation and reducing domestic credit expansion. Structurally they insist on freeing controlled prices and interest rates. They also insist on reducing trade barriers and privatization of state enterprises. It is argued in this chapter that most, if not all, of these measures are in favor of the lender rather than the borrower. These dogmatic requirements cannot possibly benefit the receiving poor countries. Each of these countries has different cultural and economic needs and values. Each country must be considered according to its own needs and capabilities.

Finally, on top of it all, the less-developed countries are internally suffering from some serious barriers to growth. Four such barriers are discussed briefly: outside competition, population explosion, lack of investment and the economic vicious cycle.

## REFERENCES

*Business Week* (2001). "Global Capitalism," January 29.

Easterly, William (2000). "The Effect of IMF and World Bank Programs on Poverty," *World Bank*, October 31, Special reports.

Friedman, Thomas L. (2000). *The Lexus and the Olive Tree*. New York: Anchor Books

Hanke, Steve H. (2000). "Abolish the IMF," *Forbes*, April 17, 84.

IMF (2001). "(HIPC) Debt Initiative," April, IMF Documents.

Malthus, Thomas, Huxley, Julian and Osborn, Frederick (1960). *Three Essays on Population*. New York: Mentor Books.

*Multinational Monitor* (1990). "Brutal Banking," April.

*Multinational Monitor* (2000). "Against IMF Realism," April.

Samli, A. Coskun (1967). "The Impact of Governmental Deficit Financing on the Growth of Underdeveloped Countries," *Mississippi Valley Journal of Business and Economics*, Fall, 68–82.

Samli, A. Coskun (1985). *Technology Transfer*. Westport, CT: Quorum Books.

# Chapter 8

# Is It Possible to be Demarginalized?

The International Monetary Fund not only refuses to admit that it has anything to do with the marginalization process discussed earlier, but it also contends that countries are not impoverished because of globalization but because of the fact that they refuse to accept the world trading system. This agency states that, in country after country, studies show that as trade increased, economies grew, incomes went up and prosperity was enhanced (Hill 2000).

However, with the exception of the Four Tigers, the IMF claims are based on averages and totals. It is possible that a country's GDP could increase along with average income, but in terms of distribution of this income, the picture could be getting worse. Indeed, this is why the WTO battle in Seattle or encounters in Genoa took place. Prescheduled conferences of representatives of the World Trade Organization, World Bank and International Monetary Fund have been confronted by very unfriendly, large groups of protesters. These protesters have different complaints but they are all against globalization. There are at least four areas of utter discontent that these protesters have articulated. (1) Some complain that globalization has taken their jobs away and given them to workers in other countries who work for very low wages. (2) Some object to globalization because they perceive it to be imperialistic. (3) Some argue against globalization because it takes away the authorities of local government. (4) Some argue bitterly against globalization because it goes against their cultural traditions. These concerns or objections caused the battle in Seattle, a confrontation in Genoa among others.

As has been discussed earlier, this is the situation in many countries, regions or companies that are being marginalized. One might think that this marginalization process should stop if everybody is getting rich. In other words, if everybody benefits from globalization, there is no marginalization. Unfortunately, this is too much to expect, and global capitalism does not have proper learnings to do something about this dismal picture.

## IS THERE SUCH A THING AS DEMARGINALIZATION?

If there is no such thing as demarginalization, then we must explore how such a concept could be developed. In particular, globalization related to financial flows is related to the demarginalization discussion. First, as Andersen Consulting discovered, it is much harder to make money when one is forced to move away from one's home market (Kraus 2000). Many countries and companies simply do not have an act they can take on the road, but are being forced to take whatever they have. This is a very dangerous proposition that typically ends in failure. Many companies from Third World countries, despite an unimpressive track record in globalization and in their home markets, are destined to accelerate their global activity further. This is due to external pressures that are perhaps unnecessary. Thus, one of the keys to demarginalization is to help companies not to succumb to the pressure to go global if they have no clear strategy for successfully participating in and capturing value through global expansion. As some companies participate in this global exercise, some people in a country will be further marginalized, since there will be only a few good jobs that will probably use high-tech rather than labor-intensive processes.

The second key area in demarginalization is distribution of the benefits of globalization. This is mainly an internal affair for the less-developed country, industry or the sector of the economy. Exhibit 8-1 presents the key aspects of this distribution concept or lack thereof. The exhibit explains that the benefits of globalization are separate from the distribution of these benefits. Whereas the benefits

Exhibit 8-1
Distribution of the Benefits of Globalization

### BENEFITS OF GLOBALIZATION

|                                      | HIGH | LOW |
|--------------------------------------|------|-----|
| **HIGH** | Most desirable demarginalization process | Demarginalization without benefits |
| **FAIR DISTRIBUTION OF BENEFITS** | | |
| **LOW** | Most noticeable marginalization | Worst case scenario – marginalization with economic stagnation |

of globalization are an externally oriented activity, distribution of these benefits is internal.

If the benefits of globalization are substantial and if these benefits are distributed equitably, then the marginalization process (if there is one) will come to a halt. This is displayed in the upper left quadrant of Exhibit 8–1.

There could be situations where the distribution of benefits would be fair but there are no benefits to speak of and, hence, there is no marginalization but there is no progress either. This is displayed by the upper right quadrant.

When the benefits of globalization are high but distribution of these benefits is less than fair, we observe excessive marginalization. Many less-developed countries in Africa, as well as India and Russia, are in this category. This situation is displayed in the lower left quadrant.

Finally, the worst case scenario is displayed in the lower right quadrant. The country does not benefit from globalization, but domestically continues marginalization because of a poor distribution of income and opportunities, and perhaps because of adverse effects of globalization that is going on elsewhere. This last point is very important in that whereas one country was involved in exporting certain raw materials, the neighboring countries may have the same opportunities. However, the neighboring countries may have become a part of globalization. By doing so they take the opportunities of exporting away from the first country. Many less-developed countries can easily fall into this trap and experience an ongoing vicious cycle of economic underdevelopment.

It is maintained here that unless the benefits of globalization are shared or the economic conditions to overcome the vicious cycle of economic underdevelopment are improved marginalization will continue. Therefore, when we think of demarginalization, we need to think just how the benefits of globalization can be distributed more equitably. We need to discuss some of the major tools of demarginalization.

## TOOLS OF DEMARGINALIZATION

Demarginalizaiton is not likely to happen all by itself. It calls for deliberate action. At least in part, it is a domestic activity and must be taken into consideration very seriously. Both private companies and national governments can, should and perhaps are participating in efforts to demarginalize. Exhibit 8–2 illustrates three sets of tools against marginalization. It must be reiterated that these are domestic tools and the exhibit does not illustrate an exhaustive list. But these tools are very important and realistic weapons against this all-out global danger of marginalization. There are three key sources of activity in demarginalization: human resource management, top corporate management, and the government of the country.

*Human resource management*: Training the workers in such a way that their productivity along with earning capacity will go up. The workers will develop new skills and will receive new knowledge which will help both the company and themselves. If such activity can take place in relatively large scales, the marginalization process can be reversed.

Similarly, enhancing worker participation in sharing the benefits of globalization can play an important role in demarginalization. Here the workers will be motivated to work harder and smarter as they become part owners of the activity. Security in conducting business and maintaining a workplace will also be increased.

*Top corporate management*: Perhaps a very important change in the orientation of top managements can be to generate a number of demarginalizaiton tools. Becoming a learning organization is one such tool. Management not only needs to be innovative in developing

**Exhibit 8-2**
**Tools of Demarginalization**

| Sources of Activity | Tools | Expected Outcomes |
|---|---|---|
| Human resource management (Micro) | Training the workers | Increased earning capacity based on skills and increase productivity |
| Shared ownership | Worker participation | Increased motivation through increased security |
| Management (Micro) | Becoming learning organization | Providing cutting edge information to the organization |
| Increasing access to knowledge | Employee appreciation | Creating the pride factor, expanding employee understanding and appreciation |
| Government (Macro) | Creating atmosphere of entrepreneurship | Increased creativity and innovation |
| Better distribution of income | Progressive income tax | Generating value for commons in the society |
| Better production environment | Heavy participation in infrastructure | Generating the foundation for better competition |
| Helping corporations | Giving direct and indirect help to companies | Contributing to demarginalization efforts |

ideas, but also must understand new technologies and be capable of staying ahead (or at least abreast) of new developments (Smythe 1999; Andolsen 1999). Such changes in orientation will provide cutting-edge information to workers of the company and increase their productivity. Gaining competitive power by becoming a learning organization, almost by definition, is a powerful demarginalization tool. Knowing as much as others or more takes away the possibility that the country, region, industry or firm will play a subservient role in the face of a powerful globalization process. This is such an important tool that it will be treated in detail in the following section.

Increasing access to knowledge and technology is certainly related to becoming a learning organization; however, it goes beyond that. It implies that not only is the organization making an effort to learn more, but also it is sharing or disseminating this information appropriately throughout the organization.

Although not totally mutually exclusive of the first two management tools, creating a sustainable competitive advantage is a critical tool to be considered. If the company can establish recognition and market power, it will contribute to employee pride that will enhance understanding, appreciation and involvement.

*Government tools*: Exhibit 8–2 identifies at least four tools that a national government can use to counteract the marginalization process. Creating an atmosphere for entrepreneurship is perhaps the most important in that group. Again, because of its special importance, this topic is also discussed further in the following section. Suffice it to say here that when conditions are suitable for entrepreneurs, it is difficult for a country to be marginalized. Entrepreneurs can start other businesses, solve other problems and contribute life to the economy that may be facing marginalization.

Progressive income tax is a must, since some people or some businesses benefit more from the current functions of the economy. But more important, if domestic enterprises are to be creative and develop new products, services or processes, there must be an appropriate infrastructure that is business-friendly. Such an infrastructure cannot be financed unless there is a progressive income tax. Without being engaged in a debate on the philosophy of taxation, it is always reasonable to think that the higher the income the lesser the value of the marginal legal tender.

Although a progressive income tax has been mentioned in conjunction with the infrastructure, it is mainly used to generate value for commons in society. Public works and commons such as parks, roads and schools are only partly held as commons and are partly infrastructure. But a major aspect of infrastructure development necessitates direct involvement of the government because infrastructure development is not profitable within itself, although it subsequently generates income as the private sector flourishes (Samli 2001).

Perhaps one of the roles of government that will be a demarginalization tool is the government's becoming directly involved in the demarginalization process. The government can help those who lose their jobs because of globalization or help companies that are at the brink of failure due to globalization. Government can open schools for retraining or make funds available for existing schools to train the people who are being marginalized.

## LEARNING ORGANIZATIONS

When Naisbitt (1982) described one of his megatrends as society moving away from an industrial society to an information society, he did not foresee the same pattern emerging through globalization. Drucker (1992) maintained that if a person wants to make a decent living in our society today, that the person can make a middle-class living only through learning and accumulating knowledge. This is also true for countries that are being marginalized. Therefore, the organizations in those countries need to become learning organizations.

In order for an organization to be considered a "learning organization," it must have a corporate culture that facilitates ideas and solutions coming from everyone in that corporation, regardless of their functions, job descriptions or locations (Hult and Ferrel 1997). These companies are proactive in making a concerted effort to get to and to stay at the cutting edge of their industry and uplift the information background of all of their employees. A brief discussion of what learning organizations are capable of and the impact of their functions is presented below. Exhibit 8–3 illustrates the key points of this discussion.

Learning organizations, above all, discover the ways they can develop effective market outreach. This activity, in return, helps the firm to establish competitive advantage and learn how to survive and even excel in global markets.

Knowledge of the firm's industry, both domestically and internationally, is essential for the learning organization. The firm can simulate some of the "best practices" in the industry or deviate from them.

The learning organization must have its key options identified and understood. This will enhance its opportunities to survive and be more profitable. The organization will be in a position to choose its best alternatives and manage accordingly.

Embracing the technology is almost an understatement. The learning organization must keep abreast with new technological developments. This activity not only will increase the firm's efficiency but will also improve its chances of establishing a competitive edge in world markets.

Information technology has been making very significant progress. The learning organization must be able to use this tool effectively. Utilization of IT implies providing proper information to the firm's employees. Effectively disseminated information throughout the firm will lead to an improved employee knowledge level.

All of the above points lead the firm toward enhancing its ability to take risks. Being able to take risks, almost by definition, will improve the firm's capability to prioritize its risk alternatives and go with

**Exhibit 8-3**
**Learning Organizations**

| Capabilities | Impact |
|---|---|
| Effective Market Outreach | Establishing competitive advantage |
| Knowledge of the Industry | Ability to simulate or deviate |
| Understanding the Company's Options | Improving survival probabilities and profit |
| Embracing Technology | Increasing efficiency |
| Learning to Use IT Effectively | Improving employee knowledge level |
| Being Able to Take Risks | Improving probability for success |
| Capitalizing on Market Opportunities | Evaluating and prioritizing market opportunities |
| Developing Additional Skills | Improving efficiency and effectiveness |
| Becoming More Proactive | Becoming more aggressive and competitive |
| Being More Entrepreneurial | Being capable of making quick far-reaching decisions |

*Source:* Adapted and revised from Smythe (1999).

the most promising ones. This attitude implies that the firm is entre-preneurial and learning. These concepts are discussed in Chapters 10 and 11.

Closely related to the ability to take risks is capitalizing on market opportunities. If the learning organization is capable of taking risks, then it can easily evaluate and prioritize market opportunities. This will keep the firm at the cutting edge of competition (see Chapter 9).

As the firm deliberately remains at the cutting edge of competition, it learns the need for additional skills and how to develop them. These skills will improve the efficiency and effectiveness of the organization.

The learning organization almost by definition becomes more proactive. It doesn't wait until things happen; it makes things happen. It essentially becomes more aggressive and, by definition, also more competitive.

Finally, being entrepreneurial implies that the firm is flexible, cre-ative and nonconventional. It can make quick decisions that are far-reaching, which will make the firm more resilient and successful.

Certainly this brief discussion of learning organizations is idealistic. However, the type of orientation described here is certainly plausible and can make a very significant difference in counteracting marginalization.

## MODERN-DAY COLONIALISM

As many poor countries are pulled into the globalization process and as worldwide capitalism progresses at its own pace and in its own way, many countries, regions and/or many groups of people are being marginalized. This author calls this process "the modern-day colonialism." The major point of this colonialism is that those who cannot keep up with this worldwide capitalism are going to fall by the wayside. In other words, while the small group of have-mores get richer, the large group of have-nothings will get larger. Should the have-mores worry about this situation? A brief analysis of human history will indicate that almost all conflicts have an economic base. The gap between the rich and the poor can become so intolerable that a conflict starts and spreads like wildfire. It may be important to realize that the 20th century was the bloodiest in the history of mankind, and all of the conflicts and wars that took place during that century had an economic base. "Economic imperialism" is another term that is used for the same phenomenon. Global capitalism makes a few very rich while it leaves many behind.

## THE PHILOSOPHY OF "KEEP YOUR POWDER DRY"

The "battle of Seattle" has already come and gone, but there are early indicators of a war against globalization. The conflict is between those who support national sovereignty against those who are for globalization and the World Trade Organization (Bagwell and Staiger 2001).

According to Sen (2001), antiglobalization protests are not altogether about globalization. The key issue is the level of inequality, and that should be our primary concern, not that it is changing marginally. If there is inequality, we must question if the distribution of benefits or economic gains through globalization is fair. The outcomes of globalization can be modified to remedy the situation. This is why the previous chapter dealt with marginalization and the present one with demarginalization. The countries that are marginalized or having difficulty as globalization gains momentum must consider not necessarily fighting off globalization but not being suckered into it helplessly. This author uses an old saying in this context: "Keep your powder dry." This entails a country maintaining its national sovereignty and trying to change some of the outcomes of globalization. Many developing countries try to modify their policies on intellectual property, investor protection, subsidies and antidumping requirements that are being imposed upon them (*The Economist* 1999). These are all demarginalization activities. Certainly a "keep your powder dry" policy can partially isolate a country from ill effects of globalization, but such a demarginalization stance adds additional cost to the country, which may be prohibitive.

It should be reiterated that globalization is very powerful and, in many cases, beneficial to only a few. It cannot be stopped; trying to stop it is going against progress. However, globalization must take a soft-landing approach rather than creating a noticeable shock effect on a country's physical, political and economic existence. It is possible, perhaps, to work more carefully with the distribution of the benefits (if any) of globalization. This is like expecting the impossible, since the outside sources and developed countries of the North American continent and the European Union simply may not approve any development along the lines of sharing the benefits of globalization more equitably.

There will be more on this topic in Chapters 9 and 10, but it must be reiterated at this point that although some countries may possibly isolate themselves from globalization, this is not necessarily in their best interest. It will indeed take the whole village (figuratively speaking) or groups of nations to decide how demarginalization may be achieved and how more equitable benefits from globalization can be obtained. In the meantime, countries experiencing marginalization must look at their individual alternatives to obtain benefits from globalization without allowing the economic conditions to get worse for certain groups or regions. Just a word about outside forces influencing the country's economy: If the country that is being marginalized can somehow be demarginalized, this will be beneficial to the lending country and to trading partners—in short, to all parties concerned and involved.

## SUMMARY

This chapter deals with demarginalization, the process by which marginalizaiton can be stopped and perhaps reversed. The chapter primarily emphasizes the internal effort of a country that is experiencing marginalization. In this respect, the opening key position is that those countries that are benefiting from globalization and capable of distributing the gains from globalization fairly, are not likely to be marginalized. Thus, one important aspect of demarginalization is internally to see to it that the gains within the country are fairly distributed.

Three key sources of demarginalization activity are discussed: human resource management, corporate top management, and the government. Through human resource management, the workers of the country can be trained further and participate in gaining benefits from globalization. Corporate top management can elect to develop learning organizations. By definition, the learning organizations perform well and typically are at the cutting edge of the industry. They create and maintain competitive advantage.

Finally, the government of the country can create the conditions whereby more entrepreneurs can emerge and work under favorable conditions created by a new and improved infrastructure. The learning organization concept is discussed in the chapter in some detail. Entrepreneurial development is such an important issue that it will be discussed in the next chapter.

## REFERENCES

Andolsen, Alan A. (1999). "Managing Digital Information," *Information Management Journal*, April, 8–15.

Bagwell, Kyle and Staiger, Robert (2001). "National Sovereignty in the World Trading System," *Harvard International Review*, Winter, 54–59.

Drucker, Peter F. (1992). *Managing for the Future*. New York: Truman Talley Books.

*The Economist* (1999). "The Battle in Seattle," November 27, 21.

Hill, Patrice (2000). "International Monetary Fund Defends Push For Globalization," Knight Ridder/Tribune Business News, April 12, 1–2.

Hult, G. Thomas and Ferrel, O.C. (1997). "A Global Learning Organization Structure and Market Information Processing," *Journal of Business Research*, 40, 155–166.

Kraus, James R. (2000). "Anderson Consulting Study Throws Some Cold Water On Globalization Strategy," *American Banker*, February, 26, 36.

Naisbitt, John (1982). *Megatrends*. New York: Warner Publishing.

Samli, A. Coskun (2001). *Empowering the American Consumer*. Westport, CT: Quorum Books.

Sen, Amartya (2001). "It's Fair, It's Good, Thoughts About Globalization," *International Herald Tribune*, July 15.

Smythe, David (1999). "Preparing New Information Professionals," *Information Management Journal*, April, 44–48.

# Chapter 9

# Needed International Entrepreneurship

In Chapter 8 it was mentioned that the countries that need and want to stop marginalization and even reverse it must use the old adage, "keep your powder dry." In other words, don't give in completely to the pressures of globalization but, even more important, try to distribute the benefits or gains from globalization more equitably. In both of these cases, developing effective entrepreneurs is one answer. Good entrepreneurs know how and when to be engaged in globalization, and they are able to earn their fair share quite reasonably. Entrepreneurship in modern times has been recognized as an engine that drives innovation and promotes economic development (Busenitz, Gomer and Spencer 2000).

Samli and Gimple (1985) stated that without inputs from entrepreneurs, economic development goals, which are particularly important to stopping marginalization, cannot be fulfilled.

With the information, technology, know-how and financial flows that have been mentioned throughout this book, less-developed countries today, more than ever before, are capable of making things and developing skills rather than expecting only the developed world to do this. Under proper conditions, the less-developed countries can carry their own weight.

It is maintained here, that more than ever before, entrepreneurial skills and technology appropriate for these skills are transferable.

LDCs do not have to develop technologies from scratch, and they do have the opportunity to acquire enough knowledge to make them suitable for their needs and capabilities. Entrepreneurs can accomplish this. Just who are these entrepreneurs?

## DEFINING ENTREPRENEURS

The French economist Richard Cantillon is said to have introduced the term *entrepreneur*. His definition was "the agent who purchased the means of production for combination into marketable products." J. B. Say expanded Cantillon's ideas. He conceptualized the entrepreneur as the organizer of the business firm. Many years later, A. S. Dewing viewed an entrepreneur as a promoter who transformed ideas into profitable business. As such, that person would have imagination, initiative, judgment and restraint. Joseph Schumpeter saw an entrepreneur as an administrator with the ability to carry new combinations of practices in running a business, including introducing new products and new methods of production, opening new markets, finding new sources of raw materials and carrying out a new organization for any industry. Over the years there have been many definitions of an entrepreneur, but there is a lack of consensus as to what the concept exactly means. In this chapter we attempt to describe the concept instead of defining it.

An entrepreneur is a highly motivated and trained person who tries to perform well, regardless of the nature of the job. He or she is an *opportunity seeker* who looks for ways to improve performance. In the process, the entrepreneur also tries to improve his or her socioeconomic status. The entrepreneur is a *decision-maker*. He or she is the person who decides on resources and skills and how much capital is needed to take advantage of certain opportunities in the marketplace. Finally, an entrepreneur is an *achiever* who takes pride in high-level performance. Some authors maintain that entrepreneurs need to achieve. Their achievement lies not only in generating ideas for a new business venture, but also in making it operational.

## HOW SHOULD INTERNATIONAL
## ENTREPRENEURS BEHAVE?

Exhibit 9–1 attempts to put together three key stages of international entrepreneurial behavior. First, certain international entrepre-

Exhibit 9-1
International Entrepreneurial Behavior Toward Value Creation

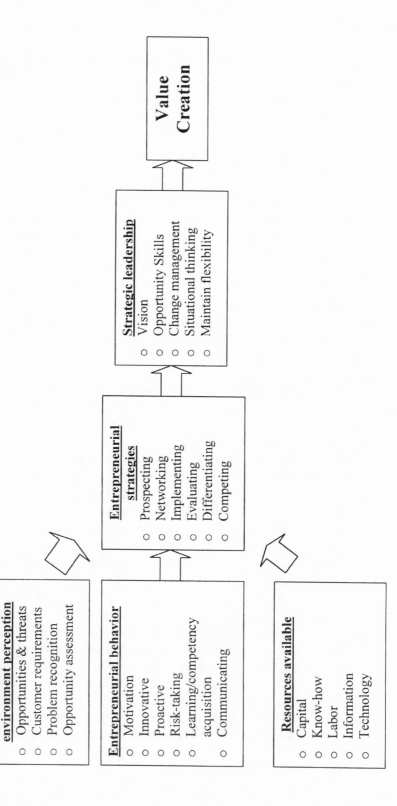

neurial behavior patterns are used to evaluate opportunities versus resources; second, based on the first phase, entrepreneurs develop important strategies; and third, they display certain strategic leadership. These three phases are discussed below.

### Business Environment, Resources and Entrepreneurial Behavior

Regarding business environment perception, entrepreneurs are likely to be in tune with opportunities and threats. They are sensitive to what is good, what is practical and what the threats are. Typically, international entrepreneurs understand customer requirements. In fact, they are perceptive enough to know what customers will require before they are actually required. This is where entrepreneurs may realize that there is a problem or there is a great opportunity. A problem may be recognized in regard to a gap where the consumer may need a product or service but doesn't quite recognize it, which is a positive problem leading to an understanding of existing market opportunities.

Recognizing customer problems implies understanding market opportunities. Entrepreneurs, almost by definition, not only recognize these opportunities but also evaluate and prioritize them. Since some businesses, particularly small businesses, cannot be engaged in many markets and lines of activity, the prioritization process is very critical. This is the only way the business that the entrepreneur is creating or running can be in the most promising and profitable activities.

The entrepreneur evaluates these opportunities further according to the resources at his or her disposal. As seen in the bottom left section of Exhibit 9–1, capital is the first resource listed. Not only all the funds available but also the borrowing power of the enterprise must be assessed. The second item is know-how. The entrepreneur always has access to information. If the existing know-how is less than adequate, the entrepreneur knows where to get the most critical information to enhance the necessary know-how level. Certainly entrepreneurs cannot do everything, they do need a few workers. These workers are carefully and personally selected and perhaps they may even become part owners. From this discussion, it is critical to connect know-how and information, with perhaps one special point noted: The workers (or partners to be) hired by the entrepreneur must be given access to the necessary information so the firm can function at the cutting edge of the industry. The entrepreneur must keep his people very well informed so they can be deeply involved in the business' affairs.

The last resource listed is technology. In this day and age, more than ever before, the entrepreneur has access to the most up-to-date technology and is capable of keeping up with it. It must be emphatically stated that the list is important but it is not ordered on the basis of priorities. Depending upon what the company is engaged in, the priority ordering of these resources can be changed dramatically.

What are the key features of the entrepreneurial behavior that make it possible to determine the opportunities and reevaluate them on the basis of available resources? The middle part of the left section in Exhibit 9–1 lists six very critical behavioral features that entrepreneurs successfully use.

Entrepreneurs are, above all, motivated to accomplish certain things. One may question just where this motivation comes from. Perhaps there is no one satisfactory answer, but the level of motivation on the part of the entrepreneur is a given and is the foundation of entrepreneurial success.

Innovativeness is also a critical entrepreneurial trait. The entrepreneur is likely to innovate new ways or improved ways of accomplishing certain business tasks. This is the only way a small business run by an entrepreneur is likely to keep up with those industrial giants who seem to have endless resources. But those giants are neither agile, flexible nor creative (Samli 2001).

Perhaps it is natural to expect proactive behavior when proper motivation and innovativeness are present. Proactive behavior implies detecting early indicators and moving very fast to make the expected changes in the market or the economy to become clear-cut benefits for the firm.

When a highly motivated, innovative and proactive entrepreneur makes certain moves, it means there are risks or there is a major risk-taking process in the making. Entrepreneurs are not wild gamblers, but they are calculated risk takers (Marcharzina 2000).

In dynamic markets and economies, risks constantly change. Hence, being involved in a continuous risk-taking activity, entrepreneurs are learning nonstop. They are acquiring competencies as new needs arise.

Finally, entrepreneurs are accomplished communicators. Not only are they involved in learning and acquiring new information, they also disseminate this information among their workers, partners and other people with whom they interact extensively.

### Entrepreneurial Strategies

Exhibit 9–1 illustrates six strategic activities for entrepreneurs. These are not alternatives. Rather, they are game plans that can improve probabilities for success. Each of these strategic activities is important for entrepreneurial success. Each activity has a strategic dimension, which can be improved by different strategic orientations.

Prospecting is the first strategy. Entrepreneurs explore new opportunities. They develop their own individualized approaches toward prospecting. Their degree of overall success rides on their prospecting strategies (Peng and Shekshina 2001). Here different entrepreneurs use different approaches. The strategy in prospecting for new opportunities can make some entrepreneurs more successful than others.

Some of the prospecting strategies dwell upon the networking strategies that entrepreneurs use. Since they cannot be a part of all of the possible networks, entrepreneurs develop their own strategies regarding networking. The networking strategy will facilitate prospecting activity by information-gathering and technology-updating.

Entrepreneurs are not only thinkers and planners but, perhaps above all, they are doers. They have the responsibility of implementing all the strategic plans (Westhead 2001). This is one of their most significant strengths. Unimplemented plans, after all, are of no value.

Not only implementing the strategies but also evaluating the results or outcomes of these strategies is an important part of entrepreneurship. A good entrepreneur has a refined ability to detect the degree of success of all of the strategies that are implemented at a very early stage in the game. These early evaluations give a second chance to some of the more refined strategies.

Almost all of the entrepreneurial strategies lead in the direction of differentiating the firm. The differentiation strategy employed by the entrepreneur can establish a competitive advantage for the firm in the marketplace. Most entrepreneurs understand this phenomenon and invariably differentiate their businesses.

Again, all of the entrepreneurial strategies enable the firm to compete more successfully. Entrepreneurs can develop their own competitive agendas to perform well in global markets. In developing and implementing these strategies, all entrepreneurs are not equally effective. Some will excel more than others. An engineering student from Turkey, whose family was involved in textiles, received a scholarship to study in Germany. In order to make some pocket money he had some samples in his bags. Some 17 years later he was employing about 10,000 people. His textile business has expanded all over Europe.

### Strategic Leadership

The third part of Exhibit 9–1 deals with the concept that some entrepreneurs excel in developing and implementing many or most of the entrepreneurial strategies. They establish a certain type of strategic leadership. There are at least five aspects of strategic leadership: vision, opportunity skills, change management, situational thinking and maintaining flexibility. Any of these, or a combination thereof, can make an entrepreneur a leader among others.

Vision is the ability to connect some specific microbusiness events to the big picture very early. It is possible for the entrepreneur to visualize that what he or she is experiencing can be a great opportunity in one corner of the world market. This is probably how the computer components production industry was developed in Malaysia.

Understanding the market well and developing special skills to evaluate opportunities can be a special strength of an entrepreneur. Again, the ability to connect microexperiences to the big picture and to evaluate the expected opportunistic outcome is a strategic leadership trait of an entrepreneur.

Entrepreneurs, almost by definition, must manage change. This is the big advantage of having a small and versatile business that is flexible enough to change as market conditions dictate. Entrepreneurs develop strategies for change management so they can successfully shift gears and move from one type of activity to another.

Strategic leadership involving vision, opportunity skills and change management all are conditioned by situational thinking. An entrepreneur is likely to assess the specific conditions within which he or she is functioning. Without a powerful situational thinking strategy, it is not possible to exercise opportunity skills, utilize vision and implement change management.

The crux of successful entrepreneurial behavior is flexibility. In one sense flexibility implies keeping options open so that the change management strategy can be implemented easily. A strategy of maintaining flexibility is therefore a necessity for successful entrepreneurial behavior.

Entrepreneurial behavior, entrepreneurial strategies and developing strategic leadership do not totally counteract marginalization activity exclusively. However, this sequence of behavior patterns, according to this author, is extremely critical for economic development, particularly in less-developed countries. As Exhibit 9–1 illustrates, entrepreneurial behavior, whether it is primarily for countermarginalization or economic development, leads in the direction of creating value for the consumer in the economy. Entrepreneurial behavior can be and perhaps must be stimulated by developing a set of conditions suitable for it. This is what is called here a "culture of entrepreneurship." The existing culture prevailing in the country must be manipulated so that a suitable aura of entrepreneurship can be created.

## DEVELOPING A CULTURE OF ENTREPRENEURSHIP

There is no perfect culture that will encourage entrepreneurship per se, or in which entrepreneurship will flourish. However, earlier studies have identified certain cultural traits, and if these traits are used in certain ways, entrepreneurship will be successful in that area. Exhibit 9–2 identifies seven traits of culture that are likely to have a direct impact on entrepreneurship. It must be reiterated that the cultural dimensions identified in the exhibit have been researched and discussed in great detail. Here, only superficially, their implications are discussed in relation to entrepreneurship. The essence of Exhibit 9–2 is validating the presence of a cultural atmosphere that can be constructed to enhance entrepreneurial performance. The first four cultural features are identified by Hofstede (1980) and the next two by Trompenaars (1994). The seventh feature is an idea recently identified by the present author.

Power distance indicates the degree of tolerance for hierarchical or unequal relationships. Particularly in Third World countries, hierarchical or unequal relationships are common. If an entrepreneur wants to work with others and to lead, he or she must be tolerant of power distances and must do whatever is needed to eliminate them to establish and maintain closeness among the workers.

Uncertainty avoidance is necessary for entrepreneurs. They must

## Exhibit 9-2
## Developing a Culture of Entrepreneurship

| Cultural Dimension | Entrepreneurial Impact |
| --- | --- |
| Power Distance – degree of tolerance for hierarchical or unequal relationship | Entrepreneurs must be tolerant of unequality but strive for equality |
| Uncertainty Avoidance – degree of acceptance for uncertainty or unwillingness to take risk | Entrepreneurs must learn to accept and work with risky propositions |
| Individualism and Collectivism – degree of emphasis placed on individual accomplishments | Entrepreneurs must work with individuals but must also acknowledge the importance of the group |
| "Musculinity" – degree of stress placed on materialism | Entrepreneurs pay only little attention to materialism and they share it with co-workers |
| Achievement – describes how power and status determined | Entrepreneurs achieve not for power per se but to make business successful |
| Universalism – describes norms for regulating behavior | Entrepreneurs determine norms of behavior to succeed |
| "Progressivism" – the degree of attention is paid to being progressive | Entrepreneurs by definition are progressive and they continue that way |

*Source:* Adapted and revised from Lee and Paterson (2000).

accept uncertainty and must be willing to take risks. Entrepreneurs must realize that they are always working with risky propositions under excessive conditions of uncertainty. The more skilled and experienced they are, the more successful they will be in avoiding uncertainty and free thinkers.

Individualism and collectivism indicate the degree of emphasis placed on the individual. Since entrepreneurs work with individuals, they must put major emphasis on individualism. They must learn to respect their workers as individuals without unrealistic risk avoidance. However, in many less-developed countries where collectivistic tendencies prevail, entrepreneurs must also acknowledge the importance of the whole group with which they are interacting.

"Musculinity" is the degree of stress placed on materialism. Entrepreneurs are not very materialistic, and whatever material gains they have, they are likely to share with co-workers. They stimulate business success along with reduced materialistic tendencies.

Achievement describes the power and status that are gained. Again, entrepreneurs are motivated to accomplish, and they achieve not in order to gain power and status per se, but to make their own business venture successful.

Universalism describes the norms for regulating behavior within the entrepreneurial undertaking. Entrepreneurs have to determine certain norms of behavior within their business concerns in order to succeed. These norms are universally applicable among all workers of the company.

"Progressivism" is the degree of attention that is paid to being progressive. Entrepreneurs must be progressive and open to new ideas so that, if necessary, they can make major adjustments to explore new ventures and take chances in areas that they have not explored before.

The existence of the cultural dimensions mentioned in Exhibit 9–2 can make a very serious difference in creating an atmosphere of entrepreneurship. Although the culture of a country or a region changes very slowly, if ever (Samli 1995), the conditions that are suitable for entrepreneurs can be somewhat manipulated by local and national governments as well as by the existing educational systems in the country. In less-developed countries, perhaps above all in Third World countries, the financial or banking system must be capable of getting entrepreneurial undertakings started. The financial backing for these ventures is not part of the culture but, without it, there could be no progress.

Just to what extent could a culture be manipulated to facilitate entrepreneurship? Knowing the features, or dimensions, of the culture, the entrepreneurial talent, somewhat individually, can be helped along the lines that are identified in Exhibit 9–2. From this perspective, if the country can help startups in the form of new businesses or new ventures, in any form, not only will the marginalization process stop, or at least be reduced substantially, but the country's economic level will rise. This is likely to happen regardless of the country's involvement in globalization. However, if noticeable globalization takes place, emergence of entrepreneurship becomes more of a necessity. In some countries, only entrepreneurs can cope with global competition that is constantly accelerating.

## SUMMARY

Entrepreneurial potential exists in all countries and all cultures. This potential must be unleashed so that marginalization can be counteracted. In fact I maintain that without entrepreneurial activity, most developing countries are not likely to make much economic progress.

This chapter deals with two extremely important topics. The first is international entrepreneurial behavior. Entrepreneurs first and foremost are motivated—they innovate, they are proactive, they take risks, they learn and they communicate. They display these behavior patterns as they determine the opportunities and match them against the resources that they have at their disposal.

Second, entrepreneurial behavior is related to the specific strategies entrepreneurs use. These strategies relate to prospecting, networking, implementing, evaluating, differentiating and, perhaps above all, competing.

The entrepreneurial strategies are critical; however, some entrepreneurs are better in implementing than others. They become strategic leaders. Those who excel in such a way have special vision, opportunity skills, change management skills, situational thinking capabilities and still can maintain a high level of flexibility.

The second part of the chapter deals with the development of a culture of entrepreneurship. If the cultural dimensions can be used in favor of developing a positive aura of entrepreneurship, this will help unleash entrepreneurial potential. Seven cultural dimensions are identified, and it is posited that, based on them, entrepreneurs must have low power distance and weak uncertainty avoidance. Moreover, they do not stress materialism, they achieve to succeed in their business, they exercise some degree of universalism and they are progressive. It is further posited that there must be financial and educational support for entrepreneurship. Perhaps more than anything else, the chapter emphasizes that entrepreneurship creates value for the society and its consumers.

## REFERENCES

Busenitz, Lowell W., Gomer, Carolina and Spencer, Jennifer W. (2000). "Country Institutional Profiles: Unlocking Entrepreneurial Phenomena," *Academy of Management Journal*, October, 994–1003.

Hofstede, G. (1980). *Culture's Consequences: International Differences in Work-Related Values.* Beverly Hills, CA: Sage.

Lee, Sang M. and Paterson, Suzanne J. (2000). "Culture Entrepreneurial Orientation and Global Competitiveness," *Journal of World Business,* Winter, 401–417.

Marcharzina, Klaus (2000). "Entrepreneurship on a Global Rise?" *Management International Review,* 3rd Quarter, 199–202.

Peng, Mike W. and Shekshina, Stanislov V. (2001). "How Entrepreneurs Create Wealth in Transition Economies," *The Academy of Management Executives,* February, 95–110.

Samli, A. Coskun (1995). *International Consumer Behavior.* Westport, CT: Quorum Books.

Samli, A. Coskun (2001). *Empowering the American Consumer.* Westport, CT: Quorum Books.

Samli, A. Coskun and Gimple, Martin L. (1985). "Transferring Technology to Generate Effective Entrepreneurs," in A. C. Samli (ed.), *Technology Transfer.* Westport, CT: Quorum Books.

Trompenaars, F. (1994). *Riding the Waves of Culture.* London: Nicholas Brealey.

Westhead, Paul (2001). "The Linkages Among Entrepreneurship, SME's and the Macroeconomy," *International Small Business Journal,* January–March, 107–112.

# Chapter 10

# Partnering Is the First Step

Chapters 8 and 9 discussed organizational learning and entrepreneurship, respectively. These are perhaps the most necessary conditions against marginalization, but not sufficient. The sufficient conditions are basically related to opening up to globalization with proper preparation. The proper preparation here is considered to be partnering and then becoming a gainful participant in certain networks. Partnering is discussed in this chapter, and network participation in Chapter 11.

As liberalization and unification activities accelerate in the European Union, corporate acquisitions have become a strong trend (Garette and Dussauge 2000). Obviously, as the globalization process accelerates, acquisitions become a more possible alternative. However, having international alliances or developing international partnerships and creating fruitful partnering relationships have been rather popular and successful globally. There is, therefore, the choice of alliances versus acquisitions.

In the face of accelerated globalization activity, should the Third World countries resort to opting for partnerships, or should they try to be acquired by a foreign parent company? Exhibit 10–1 contrasts the benefits or advantages of alliances versus acquisitions.

**Exhibit 10-1**
**Alliances versus Acquisitions**

| Alliance Benefits | Acquisitions Benefits |
|---|---|
| o Complimentary capabilities | o Short-run financial benefits |
| o Reversible to previous state | o More economies of scales |
| o Partners are free of being forced to make certain decisions | o Simpler to make decisions |
| o Partners remain independent | o Faster to move on into complicated problem areas |
| o Complimentary alliances support offensive strategies | o Strong defensive strategies |

## ALLIANCES

If firms want to join forces, they pool their assets, combine their resources and develop joint synergies. They can collaborate in specific and well-defined areas and still maintain their autonomy. As such, alliances are more capable of planning for and taking advantage of alliances based on complementarity of their capabilities (Garette and Dussauge 2000). Of course, alliances can last as long as partners desire. They are reversible. If the partners deem to dissolve the partnership, they can do so any time they desire.

Similarly, partners in alliances can choose not to go along with the others. If they do not wish to undertake, perform or continue with certain operations, they are free to follow their own minds or consciences. Partners in alliances, therefore, remain free. Independence makes it more attractive for them to join an alliance. If the alliance they join does not offer benefits or does not make a synergistic contribution to their well-being, then they don't have to remain in that relationship.

As has been implied thus far, complementary relationships that are synergistic support offensive or competitive strategies. Because of the nature of these alliances, they can change strategies and, they can change their competitive posture somewhat dramatically.

## ACQUISITIONS

Particularly in the United States and Japan, acquisitions have been the primary mode of activity. Above all, they rely on scale economies and short-run financial benefits. They achieve this goal by generating minimum efficient output levels (Garette and Dussauge 2000).

Of course, when companies are acquired, it is easy to eliminate excess capacities, duplications and costly operations. Although at times dictatorial, it is simple to make decisions. This is because in acquisitions, partners do not maintain their personality and independence. The newly acquired firm has to follow the orders of the new master.

Closely related to the simplicity of making decisions, in acquisitions it is much faster to undertake solutions in complicated problem areas. Again, since the individual partners do not have independence, they have to go along with decisions generated at headquarters.

Finally, acquisitions are used for defensive purposes. They reduce competition and enhance cost effectiveness. As a result, they assert themselves in the market against reduced and perhaps less-efficient competition.

Although both alliances and acquisitions have their own attractions, in terms of helping Third World countries, alliances may be considered more beneficial. Acquisitions in these countries are somewhat like foreign direct investments. They can take out more than they put in, and they can pull out as suddenly as they entered. Moreover, their cost-efficiency approaches may cause more layoffs than the benefits of foreign investments the countries may be receiving. Furthermore, in cases of acquisition, there is no assurance that the nationals will not be replaced by the acquisition country's expatriates. In other words, if Company A in a Third World country is purchased by Company B from another country that is more economically advanced, then Company A executives and managers may be replaced by Company B employees. Finally, in cases of acquisition, there are no independent partners remaining; hence, there may not be a foundation for requesting financial equality and technology transfer. Thus alliances provide more leverage to Third World countries and companies from those countries.

Although there is much partnering and acquisition activity going on in developed and newly industrialized countries, the details of needed partnerships for the emerging or Third World countries are not quite established. One may examine the needs of companies from both emerging and developed countries so that certain common denominators can be established that will be beneficial to both parties in their search for suitable partnerships.

In the first section of this chapter, we made a case for the possibility of partnering as a way to enter into globalization activity without being marginalized. Here it is argued that partnering, rather than acquisitions or direct investments, is more desirable for the emerging countries. Since companies from these countries are looking for partners in order to become a part of the globalization process, their needs must match those companies from developed countries that are looking for partners. If we analyze both parties' preferences, then we will identify common denominators, if there are any. These common denominators will enhance the cooperation between the parties and will make the partnership long-lived.

## PRIORITIES OF COMPANIES FROM EMERGING COUNTRIES

Exhibit 10–2 illustrates priorities that companies from emerging and developed countries have in their partner selection. Companies from emerging markets can adjust their priorities somewhat so that they can participate in globalization. Five specific priorities are cited: assets, capabilities, expertise-sharing, quality performance and access to globalization.

Obviously, one of the most important features of a future partner from the perspective of a Third World firm is financial assets. These companies need financial help so they can expand and become economically viable in the global setting.

If the prospective partner does not have certain technical capabilities, it is not worthy of partnership. Companies from emerging countries are interested in organizational learning as discussed in Chapter 8.

However, having certain technical capabilities, or expertise, and sharing them are not the same thing. Companies of the Third World need to receive certain expertise so they can become more viable in the race for globalization or against the threats of globalization. This is part of the technology transfer that is discussed earlier in Chapters 3 and 8. The prospective partner must have the skills to transfer technology successfully.

Not only technical capabilities and willingness to share them, but the prospective partner must have capacity for quality. Here the term "capacity" implies that the prospective partner not only believes in and practices quality in its activities, but also tries to expand this quality dimension. The prospective partner should be in constant search for better quality in its products and services. Similarly, this partner-to-be must be at the cutting edge of the industry so that new levels of expertise can be achieved by the firms from emerging economies.

Perhaps above all, what the company from a Third World country needs from a prospective partner is to gain access to the global network. If the prospective partner has been reasonably successful in global trade, it may be able to carry the Third World company into the globalization process. The company from the Third World cannot accomplish successful globalization all by itself.

## PRIORITIES OF DEVELOPED MARKET FIRMS

There are also five priorities for developed firms: leveraging resources, unique competencies, market knowledge, attractiveness and cost benefits. Leveraging resources for companies from developed markets implies diversifying their sources of supplies as well as their investments. Thus the inclination to leverage their resources may attract companies from developed countries to financially more-well-off firms or to those that have a very strong market position.

Companies from developed markets may also seek prospective partners with some unique competencies. Such partnerships would help these firms to diversify their market offerings or produce their products more efficiently. These skills may give the companies some synergistic benefits by making them better performers in the marketplace. Local market knowledge and access to these markets could be very attractive to the firms from developed markets that are booking prospective partners. Many Japanese, American or European companies that are thinking of entering a market may find it convenient to partner with some companies that have familiarity with and have been functioning well in these markets. In other words, they can provide access into these markets for their partners-to-be.

Some industries are more attractive than others for the companies from developed countries that are looking for partners. This attractiveness may be displayed by at least three possible avenues. First, the company from a developed market may find a prospective partner that can regularly provide high-quality raw materials or parts. This arrangement can improve its productive facility utilization because of a steady supply of raw materials; it also can improve its quality of the finished products due to controlled and probably improved raw ma-

**Exhibit 10-2**
**Priorities for International Partner Selection**

| Priorities of Emerging Market Firms | Priorities of Developed Market Firms |
|---|---|
| o  Financial assets | o  Focus on leveraging resources |
| o  Technical capabilities | o  Unique competencies |
| o  Willingness to share the expertise | o  Local market knowledge and access |
| o  Capacity for quality | o  Industry attractiveness |
| o  Will carry the company into globalization | o  Cost benefits |

*Source:* Adapted and revised from Hitt et al. (2000).

terials or parts. Second, the company from a developed market may be looking for a partner in an industry that it aspires to enter itself. That gives the firm an opportunity to enter into the industry easily and perhaps test its effectiveness before it enters some larger markets in a big way. Finally, the firm seeks partners in the same industry to gain more market power globally. This approach can allow the company to grow faster than its competitors in a fast-growing industry.

Almost all of these priorities can generate cost benefits. However, the firm from a developed market may be looking for a partner particularly for cost advantages. Cost leadership may be that firm's key strategic thrust, and the firm may be trying to enhance that advantage by cutting costs further through the help of a partner.

As can be seen in Exhibit 10–2, the priorities of these two groups are significant but different. However, there are situations where, while the priority for the emerging country is having the firm satisfied, in that the partner will carry the company into globalization, simultaneously, that company will provide cost benefits for its partners from a developed country. Obviously, the firms from countries that are being marginalized through globalization may have to try harder to look more attractive to their partners-to-be in developed countries.

## HOW TO ENTER INTO A PARTNERSHIP

American firms are anxious to arrange partnerships with Chinese firms so they can enter this ever-growing market. Simultaneously,

Chinese partners can give cost benefits. However, it is not so easy to enter into a partnership with Chinese companies. First, most local partners are state-owned and hence controlled by the Chinese government. The Chinese government could have different motives than, say, maximizing profits. Second, Chinese partners may be very keen to learn from their American partners, but they do not have the same concepts of efficiency or competition (Calantone and Zhao 2001). Third, they don't give control opportunities to their American partners, even though these American partners can perform much better when they have more control.

Similar and more varied desires and demands make it difficult to enter into an international partnership. In very general terms, first, the criteria for the partnership need to be established—that is, who is going to do what, how and for what reason. Second, the connections should be developed. Finding the right partner is a challenging, costly and, above all, risky activity that needs to be performed carefully. If this connection function cannot be performed satisfactorily up front, very little is likely to be accomplished subsequently. In fact, this is why many intended partnerships fail very quickly. Typically they do not do enough research on the prospective partners early on. The rules of the partnership also have to be established very early if the partnership is expected to live and prosper. The rules may indicate who will do what, the strategic orientation of the partnership, how evaluation and control functions will be established and, if necessary, how the partnership will be dissolved. Many other details could be included in the rules of the partnership. Finally, the partnership agreement may include different alternatives that may vary from which markets or products and services to concentrate on in their overall production. Perhaps the most critical areas of concern here are how the alternatives are evaluated and prioritized, and, what would prompt moving from one alternative to the next.

## LEARNING FROM PARTNERS

As was discussed in Chapter 8, learning is important to both parties in a partnership. However, all organizations are not learning organizations and, hence, they are not exactly proactive in recognizing the importance of learning and acting as good learning organizations typically function. Companies from the countries that are being marginalized have to be learning organizations no matter what. Only with such an attitude can they counteract marginalization.

## BACK TO TECHNOLOGY TRANSFER

One of the most critical features of globalization, as stated in Chapter 3, is technology transfer. For the technology to be truly successfully transferred, the receiver must be a learning organization. In addition, the receiver should be entrepreneurial, so that not only will the technology be transferred successfully, but it also will be changed, adjusted and made less costly, more effective or whatever, to make it more suitable for the receiver's market. It must be reiterated that without globalization such transfer of technology would not be possible. But it is up to the recipient to make good use of the newly transferred technology. It is this author's belief that successfully transferred technology can have a ripple effect, meaning that the lessons learned from one industry can be extremely useful to other industries as well. Some of the domestic industries that have not gotten a boost through direct technology transfer can learn to improve by indirect lessons received from other technology transfer processes. This ripple effect can be a very significant countermarginalization weapon (Samli 1985).

## PARTNERING OR ALLIANCE OPPORTUNITIES

In this chapter, we have treated partnering and alliances interchangeably. It is important to realize that all countries or all companies do not have equal capabilities. Similarly, they may not even have the same opportunity to develop alliances or partnerships. Exhibit 10–3 illustrates this situation.

The upper left quadrant of Exhibit 10–3 indicates the situation all firms, industries and countries should have as a goal. Here the opportunities to create working partnerships or alliances are high. If the finding and organizing skills for such alliances are also high, then there will be a great opportunity for such alliances to be beneficial to all parties concerned, and to be especially beneficial to the countries that are being marginalized or trying hard to develop their economies.

The lower left quadrant indicates the presence of opportunities, but the firm, industry or the country is not able to take advantage of the situation. There should be an unbiased and capable organization in

**Exhibit 10-3**
**Skills versus Opportunities**

ALLIANCE FINDING OPPORTUNITIES

|  | HIGH | LOW |
|---|---|---|
| HIGH<br><br>ALLIANCE<br>FINDING<br>SKILLS | Good opportunity for mutual benefit | Possible opportunity with lack of substance |
| LOW | Needed outside help<br>Lost opportunity | No opportunity for progress<br>Need a major modification of conditions |

the world to help those who can take advantage of the situation by bringing parties together.

The upper right quadrant indicates the situation where alliance-finding skills are high, but opportunities are not available. In such cases there is some opportunity, but ambition is not enough. It will be necessary to develop some opportunities by perhaps emphasizing the development of certain *attractive* industries.

Finally, the lower right quadrant displays the most difficult situation, where the opportunities as well as the capabilities are not present. In such cases, the firm, industry or country truly needs economic aid. Once again, such aid needs to be administered by a neutral world organization that is not driven by profit motive or the benefit of the investors, as may be in the case of the International Monetary Fund or the World Bank.

## SUMMARY

This chapter advocates that partnering is an important first step to nullify or reduce the marginalization process. First, it is argued that developing alliances is better than being purchased by a company from the developed markets of the world. If an alliance were to be developed, selecting a partner becomes a critical issue. Here companies from emerging markets and developed markets have different orientation and motivation. Companies from emerging markets should be more proactive and accommodating.

In order to develop strong partnerships, four areas must be emphasized: criteria, connections, rules, and alternatives. It is further argued that establishing good functional partnerships should go back to technology transfer and the development of learning organizations. Companies, industries or countries of emerging markets must emphasize these two vital areas.

Finally, the chapter identifies four separate conditions related to having or not having alliance opportunities, along with the skills to develop them.

## REFERENCES

Calantone, Roger J. and Zhao, Yushan Sam (2001). "Joint Ventures in China: A Comparative Study of Japanese, Korean and U.S. Joint Ventures," *Journal of International Marketing*, January, 1–16.

Garette, Bernard and Dussauge, Pierre (2000). "Alliances Versus Acquisitions: Choosing the Right Option," *European Management Journal*, February, 63–69.

Hitt, Michael A., Dacin, M. Tina, Levitas, Edward, Edhec, Jean-Luc Arregle and Borza, Anca (2000). "Partner Selection in Emerging and Developed Market Contexts: Resource-Based and Organizational Learning Perspectives," *Academy of Management Journal*, June, 449–467.

Samli, A. Coskun (1985). *Technology Transfer*. Westport, CT: Quorum Books.

# Chapter 11

# Partnerships Expand into Networks

Learning from a partner from emerging markets that has good intentions and can work smoothly with the company is putting the best foot forward. When Nokia, the major cell phone producer, looks for a partner or partners to source parts of the phone, globally or totally built in another country, there are opportunities for companies from emerging markets to partner with Nokia. Similar arrangements have been going on in other industries and countries.

In Chapter 10, it was discussed that companies in Third World countries can get into a partnership arrangement and, by using entrepreneurship and learning organization approaches in these partnership situations, they may be able to counteract the marginalization that globalization is bringing about. Partnership arrangements are the first step in that direction. But it does not simply stay there. As globalization accelerates, a special interest in networks starts fueling and, out of that, what some call value networks emerge (Allee 2000). Such a value network is likely to generate economic progress by using complex and dynamic exchange systems composed of a number of enterprises, customers, suppliers, strategic partners and even the whole community (Allee 2000). Network organizations are independent coalitions of task- or skill-based economic entities. They typically do not have hierarchical control. They thrive on mutuality and reciprocity in a shared value system that identifies the roles and responsibilities of

**Exhibit 11-1**
**Membership Progression**

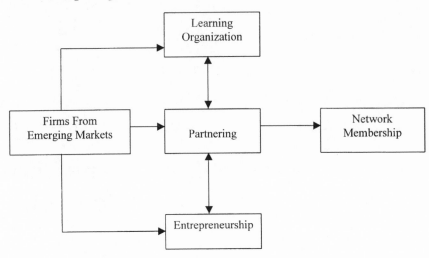

their numbers (Achrol and Kotler 1999). They construct a series of value exchanges that would improve the performance of all parties involved and similarly would benefit all parties that are part of the network.

## BEING IN A NETWORK GIVES SECURITY

Firms from emerging markets may first seek to become involved in partnering. But the membership progressions should not stop there if they want to reverse marginalization and take full advantage of globalization. They should become members of value networks. Such networks provide additional security for these firms, which probably already are members of partnerships at this point.

Exhibit 11–1 illustrates the membership progression of a company from emerging markets in search of countermarginalization. Those who are in the process of partnering, and who exercise organizational learning and entrepreneurship, start looking for expansion into a network membership.

## NETWORKS ARE DETERRENT PLUS

Peter Drucker (1992) has described the economy of the future as a network society. Networks are not necessarily new, but they have not found their rightful place in emerging or less-developed countries where they are now needed.

A network is an institutional affiliation among firms that operate in a number of related and unrelated industries that may center around a bank and a trading company. It has shared resources and shared strategic decisions (Achrol and Kotler 1999). It engages in more than simple transactions around goods, services and revenue. It generates flows among members (Allee 2000). Four distinct flows take place within a network:

1. Goods, services and revenue flows. Networks create a flow of transactions, contracts, invoices, orders received and requests for proposals. All the products and knowledge of products are basically part of the product and service exchange.
2. Knowledge flows: These contain strategic information, planning knowledge, process knowledge, technical know-how and more.
3. Intangible benefit flows: Special benefits such as image enhancement, customer loyalty, co-branding, among others, are included here.
4. Intermarket flows: Networks may be designed to take advantage of intermarket opportunities regarding increasing demand, improved production opportunities and the like (Allee 2000; Achrol and Kotler 1999; Anderson 2000).

Thus, networks composed of partners, keyed to external competition, particularly coming from developed markets, can create the possibility of counteracting marginalization. In fact, as can be seen, networks truly provide the opportunity to become a part of and take advantage of globalization. As the networks emerge and start trading jointly, they create trading network blocs. Exhibit 11–2 illustrates such a situation showing six networks. Each network jointly and/or individually may be involved in trade. The network will enable individual firms that would otherwise be marginalized to become gainful participants in trade relationships. Thus, networks are more than just countermarginalization. They enhance trading opportunities.

## SUCCESS FOR NETWORKS

It is maintained here that if companies from emerging markets first partner and then network with others, and if these networks can hold

**Exhibit 11-2**
**Networks Expand into Blocs**

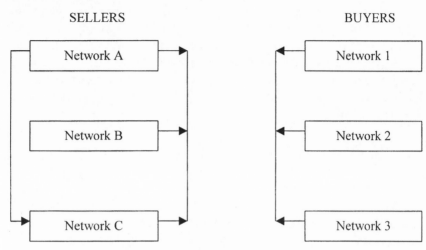

their own as trading blocs, then not only will marginalization be counteracted, but there will be widespread benefits.

Success for networks relies heavily on better distribution of the benefits of globalization. Companies, regions and countries will not be overlooked if successful trading network blocs are functioning in the world markets and generating value and wealth for those who otherwise would be have-nothings. But how will these networks function so they will be successful? Regardless of the makeup of the network, be it partnership, strategic alliance or joint venture, it is critical that it perform numerous functions. Exhibit 11–3 illustrates at least six such functions. The network may be seeking international sourcing for its finished products or to supply raw or semifinished products.

The network may successfully transfer technology because the labor costs or raw materials costs may be low and, hence, producing the products of this alliance in the new partner locations may be more beneficial for the competitiveness of the whole network. One member of the network may be an insider in the market to which the network is aiming. That partner will be very helpful to the total network by helping the network successfully function in that market. One or more members of the network may be financially very fit or may have a very good credit rating. Certainly, if the network has more money and can use that money effectively, the whole network will do well. Those members who lack financial capability will benefit from the network.

Exhibit 11-3
Network Functions Leading to Trading Blocs

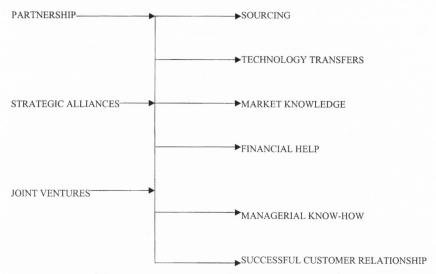

What has been implied thus far is that the network has to have managerial know-how. If none of the partners have managerial know-how, the whole network is likely to fail. It is therefore of the utmost importance that some member in the network exercise good management practices. Finally, if the members of the network have been successful in keeping their customers happy, they can teach others all about good customer relationships. If and when the whole network of members learns to practice good customer relationships, then the whole group is likely to benefit.

Successful customer relationships will enable the whole network to trade with one another. Whereas there are not too many country-by-country trading arrangements, there are numerous location-by-location, city-by-city or group-of-company by group-of-company trading arrangements. Any one of these can easily counteract marginalization and create economic growth for the parties involved. It is, however, not very clear how networks and trading blocs emerge.

## HOW TO BE SOLICITED INTO A NETWORK

Partner selection processes by companies in emerging and developed markets have been described and contrasted. However, partnering is not enough. Trading networks of different types and scopes are necessary. There is no one best way that a company from a Third World country would automatically be solicited to participate in an emerging or already functional network. Selection of partners by networks will call for *willingness* and *flexibility* on both sides. After all, if the network is not composed of certain firms with certain capabilities, it will not be viable as it faces other networks or trading blocs in the world markets. It is obvious that all participants must be learning organizations and willing to exercise entrepreneurial orientation toward excelling in the competitive arena where they function. Certainly they must be flexible enough to change dramatically if and when needed.

When both sides are willing and flexible, they certainly have a good opportunity to locate partners to participate in trading networks. Although there is no one perfect way of soliciting or being solicited for a network, with current developments in computerized international communication, it is becoming easier to put together networks that become trading blocs. When a network functions as a trading bloc, it must be in a position to coordinate its activities and create a synergistic personality that will be recognized, liked and respected.

There are a number of other conditions that need to exist for the network to function effectively. Among these are: (1) bilateral communications, (2) ability to question decisions, (3) full knowledge of the final decision, (4) consistency in the decision-making process, and (5) familiarity with local conditions (Ellis 2000).

Bilateral communications imply that the network participants freely share perceptions, knowledge, expertise and ideas that are critical for the network's strategy development. This is done anytime, anywhere, by anybody within the network system.

All participants in the network must have the freedom and opportunity to question decisions regarding the network's functions and strategy implementation.

A full knowledge of final decisions primarily related to the network's competitiveness and strategic posture must be made available to all members of the network. Thus the participants would appreciate the activities that are taking place.

Consistency in the decision-making process means that there is no political favoritism within the network and that no one partner gets unwarranted and undue favors or special treatment. Hence, there exists a level playing field.

Finally, wherever the network action regarding market competitiveness and strategy implementation take place, there is a full level of familiarity with these localities. The conditions that prevail in these locations, or markets, are well known to the members of the network.

It is clear that networks can play an important role in counteracting the marginalization process and even reversing it. But becoming a part of a network is not a given. It does not happen automatically; it must be earned. Furthermore, individual firms must understand their role within the network and the role of the total network so that there will be a good match.

## A MAJOR MACROMARKETING JOB

As firms become part of networks and further parts of trading blocs, they not only take care of themselves against marginalization as a result of globalization, but also strengthen the group of companies, regions or countries economically. In other words, trading blocs or networks are likely to make a major contribution to the economic well-being of people in that country.

We may think, for instance, of a poor region in Turkey where a group of small textile firms has created a network. They expand their network by connecting with a group of German importers. They create a trading bloc. But it will take the willingness and flexibility we talked about earlier. The whole region will pitch in to create the success and continuity of this arrangement. The network, in time, may expand to include other countries or some businesses from other countries.

Here, participating companies will have to evaluate and protect their own benefits as well as local or regional economic benefits. In other words, they will be concerned not only with micromarketing, but with macromarketing as well, because it will provide economic synergy, say, for the whole region. Thus the trading networks become "value nets" and generate consumer value, which, of course, is the essence of countermarginalization.

## ACTIVITIES WITHIN AND BETWEEN BLOCKS

Individual firms find partners, develop networks and become trading blocs. This progression is shown in Exhibit 11–1. In Exhibit 11–3, network functions leading to the emergence of blocs was illustrated. Exhibit 11-4 deals with important internal and external activ-

**Exhibit 11-4**
**Trading Blocs in Internal and External Activities**

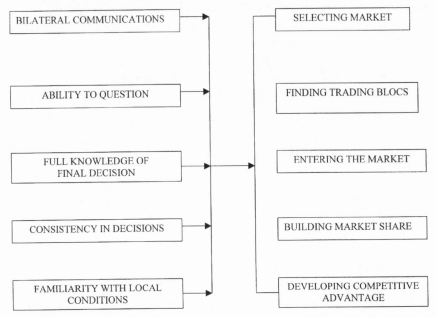

ities of successful trading blocs. The internal activities were briefly discussed earlier; a brief discussion of external activities is presented here.

The trading bloc that wants to become a reality is a network that must have at least the five major external activities presented in Exhibit 11–4: (1) selecting the market, (2) finding the trading bloc, (3) entering the market, (4) building market share and (5) developing competitive advantage. We cannot maintain that this is an all-inclusive list. However, it is a very important and necessary list of functions to consider and put to use, if any success is expected in creating sustainable trading blocks.

The network is primarily engaged in identifying the market that is most likely to have networks or trading blocs that may be suitable for developing sustainable trading relationships. Being able to identify and prioritize the prospective potential markets is the most critical first step.

Within the identified target market, finding the exact network that will trade is not quite so easy. This author believes that the days of grandiose trade agreements among groups of nations are gone. Instead, there will be small local networks (or alliances) which will establish good trading relationships among or between regions or nations.

Once partners, networks and blocs are identified and organized, entering the target market may not be difficult. Knowing enough international marketing and providing the right type of products and services in the manner the market desires all can be accomplished if the trading blocs manage to create working relationships with other trading blocs (Samli and Hill 1998).

Building market share may be more difficult than the entry. Here the trading blocs or networks will have to be more sensitive to niches in the market. Niche marketing or catering to unusual demands of a small but well-identified portion of a small market is perhaps the most desirable and realistic approach that companies from less-developed countries and their partners from developed countries may successfully accomplish (Kotler, Jatusripitak and Maesincee 1997).

For a sustainable relationship to emerge, the networks or blocs need to establish competitive advantage. This is primarily based on the network's capabilities and workings. It has been maintained here that networks are particularly important in knowledge-intensive industries or other industries where demand uncertainty is strong but reasonably stable supply chains exist. The network can generate much flexibility and speed (Moe 2001). These features will generate competitive advantage.

The number of alliances and networks is growing at an estimated rate of 25 percent per year. As these interorganizational relationships increase in numbers and outreach, they create value for the regions involved and for the networks but, above all, for the countries in question that are struggling against the marginalization process (Moe 2001).

Giants such as Nike, Intel or Toyota have used alliances or networks very successfully. In fact, much of their success in global markets can be attributed to these alliances or networks (Bovel and Martha 2000). There is no reason why small Third World companies cannot do the same in certain smaller or niche markets.

## SUSTAINABLE NETWORKS

It is critical that the networks or trading blocs be sustainable and that they last a long time and continue benefiting their economies.

The internal and external activities of these business complexes (Exhibit 11–4) must be performed in such a way that there will be coordination within the groups so that each member knows what needs to be done and when. Of course, such coordination cannot come about unless there is effective communication with the group. Similarly, as was implied earlier, there must be direction or goals for the group. These goals must be met in the present time and, if needed, be changed in the future.

It is critical to realize that although such networks or trading blocs are successful, many such interorganizational relationships also go out of existence. Consistency in their performance and continuity in their existence are not automatic, and they call for much effort on the part of both the participants and the whole system. But if they survive, they can generate value for all parties concerned as well as for the economies of the countries involved.

## SUMMARY

It is critical for companies in emerging markets to establish or become a part of partnerships, networks and trading blocs. In order to accomplish this, these companies must have entrepreneurial orientation and must be learning organizations. They could have partnerships, strategic alliances or joint ventures. Whichever arrangement they can manage, that arrangement must be able to accomplish the following: sourcing, transfer technology, market knowledge, financial help, managerial know-how and strong customer relationship. The networks that want to become trading blocs must have certain internal and external activities. Internally, they must have bilateral communication, ability to question, full knowledge of final decision, consistency in these decisions and familiarity with local markets.

Externally, they must be able to select markets, find trading blocs, enter the market, build market share and develop competitive advantage. Thus, coordination and communication in these groups are very critical for their success and continuity. In addition to coordination and communication, cooperation and competency are required for sustainable and successful arrangements.

## REFERENCES

Achrol, Ravi S. and Kotler, Philip (1999). "Marketing in the Network Economy," *Journal of Marketing*, January, 146–163.

Allee, Verna (2000). "Reconfiguring the Value Network," *The Journal of Business Strategy*, July/August, 36–39.

Anderson, Shirley C. (2000). "The Globally Competitive Firm: Functional Integration Value Chain Logistics, Global Marketing and Business College Strategic Support," *Competitiveness Review*, March, 33–45.

Bovel, David and Martha, Joseph (2000). "From Supply Chain to Value Net," *The Journal of Business Strategy*, August, 24–28.

Drucker, Peter F. (1992). *Managing for the Future*. New York: Truman Talley Books.

Ellis, Kimberly M. (2000). "Strategic Contexts, Knowledge Flows, and the Competitiveness of MNCs: A Procedural Justice Approach," *Competitiveness Review*, January, 9–24.

Kotler, Philip, Jatusripitak, Somkid and Maesincee, Suvit (1997). *The Marketing of Nations*. New York: The Free Press.

Moe, Michael J. (2001). "Creating Value Through Working with Others: Interorganizational Relationships," *The Academy of Management Executive*, February, 150–152.

Samli, A. Coskun and Hill, John S. (1998). *Marketing Globally*, Lincolnwood, IL: NTC Books.

# Proactive Defense Mechanism

When Friedman (2000) draws a parallel between globalization and being run over by an electronic herd, he sets the tone of defense mechanisms that the Third World countries will have to develop to defend themselves against marginalization or being run over by the electronic herd. It is obvious that this electronic herd can be counteracted by a counterattack, which will have to be a proactive defense mechanism with perhaps multiple dimensions. A simple reactive strategy will not provide the defense that is needed. Again, using Friedman's concept, the electronic herd simply does not come and stay at the border of the country. It enters uncontrollably, and the winner takes all. Hence the country has too much at stake to handle the situation with a slow reactive strategy which may be ineffective because it may be too little too late.

But above all, with the four flows discussed earlier—capital, information, technology and know-how—less-developed countries have a chance to prepare their development strategies. These strategies must be proactive in that these countries will establish their own development scenarios rather than simply responding to others since, as has been in evidence thus far, there simply is not one wonderful formula that benefits all countries equally well. Such scenarios will, by definition, prevent the marginalization process that follows globalization. This may be construed as a defense strategy. But it is critical to think not of just defending oneself against globalization. If a defensive posture against globalization is in effect, countries will try to keep it from entering. Such defensive posture will go in the direction of protectionism. And if such a stance succeeds, the spectacular benefits that will accrue from globalization will remain out of the country. This is a total deprivation that will worsen economic positions.

However, taking all that globalization has to offer and using these benefits for a proactive strategy development is a much better approach. This approach will provide the needed defense without depriving the country of the benefits of globalization.

## PROACTIVE DEFENSE

Friedman (2000) points out that there are large groups that object to globalization. He calls them "backlash demagogues." These groups, according to Friedman have simple solutions and actually would like to slow down or stop the process completely. Some of these people were engaged in the battle in Seattle or confrontations in Genoa. But, it must be understood that the impact (at times devastating) of globalization is not simply subject to demagoguery but is very real. In fact, it will not only be naïve to think that only demagogues are objecting to globalization, but it will be rather dangerous. Such misinterpretation of the problem will simply lead in the direction of wrong remedies.

The position taken here is not protectionistic per se; rather, it is proactivity. It is true that there are those who do not want their cultures to be invaded and perhaps even eliminated. It is also true that globalization is a major American initiative and, as such, there are objections to it. There are groups of people around the world who do not like anything related to the United States or anything that might be coined "American." Furthermore, in most Third World countries (or even in others), there is a power structure that is being undermined by globalization. As a result, many local governments are losing their authority or power. Certainly, those who are losing stature in their own countries because of globalization are not thrilled with that concept. Many societies have those traditionalists who do not like change. Because globalization brings about change, they are against it. All of these groups would like to stop globalization. But such a move would be a terrible deprivation for these societies. It is questionable if they could truly develop their economies without being open to the world. If the Chinese "cultural revolution" were to be used as an example, during which China was closed to the outside world and made no economic progress, it easily can be said that without globalization and related trade activity, other countries cannot make it either.

## THE FOUR TIGERS ONCE MORE

The Four Tigers have not tried to stop globalization. On the contrary, they have made a concerted effort to take advantage of the opportunities that globalization provided for them. But they did not act defensively to protect something, be it some tradition or existing power structure. They not only took advantage of the globalization process but got ahead of the movement itself (Kotler et al. 1997). These countries not only used a proactive approach to economic development by being ahead of globalization activity but also were quite reasonable in distributing the benefits of their progress to all of their people. What the Four Tigers have accomplished is the construction of their own unique economic development strategies in a very proactive manner. The results have been extremely impressive.

## THE BEST DEFENSE IS AN OFFENSE

For those societies or regions that are concerned about marginalization, the idea is not the old-fashioned protectionism of keeping foreign competition, foreign capital and foreign goods and services out of the country, but using these and other opportunities to take full advantage of globalization. In such cases, possibilities of marginalization are eliminated by proactive economic strategies that use global opportunities to the limit, as has been seen on the part of the Four Tigers. This implies in an obvious way that the best defense indeed is an offense. Proactivity is much more desirable to reactive postures that may turn out to be reactionary, such as strong protectionism. And protectionism is likely to deprive the country of many major benefits of globalization by keeping it out of the country. The important point, obviously, is to take advantage of globalization as well as to protect against some of its very strong negative influences. This is where the best defense is an offense. The country, region or industry can move in the direction of becoming a part of globalization (offense) but make sure that it will not cause marginalization (defense). Such an end can be reached by developing a proactive growth strategy.

## A PROACTIVE GROWTH STRATEGY

Exhibit 12–1 presents a proactive growth strategy. Parts of this strategy, or the game plan, have been already developed in previous chapters. Constructing it by putting the pieces together is very critical because then the model makes it possible to see the whole picture. This exhibit is based on a model originally developed by Thurow (1999), modified by this author in an earlier book (Samli 2001) and finally further modified for this book. There are eight key points to the model. Some of these points are further elaborated upon in the next chapter.

The first and perhaps most basic step in the model is creating and maintaining public order. Particularly in less-developed countries, lack of political stability does not allow for the economy to blossom. Indeed, almost in all countries where public order and/or political stability are not present, the economy starts deteriorating. Many developing countries get so involved in party politics that one questions if that is the only way or the best way to proceed. Without the public order proviso, it is almost impossible to construct and maintain the necessary infrastructure. Japan, Taiwan and Singapore, in the most recent decades, have managed to put much emphasis on their infrastructures and that, in turn, accelerated their economic growth further. Additionally, the first basic step requires the organization and staffing of schools as well as the delivery of adequate services. Without these essentials, it will be almost impossible for the society to make any progress.

The second step is related to borrowing international funds wisely and using these monies in critical investment areas to increase productivity and generate valuable output by investing in factories, equipment and housing.

Enhancing entrepreneurship and organizational learning is very critical. It is necessary to create proper conditions so that entrepreneurs and learning organizations will flourish. Without such conditions, it will be unreasonable to expect great performance from the economy.

Creating opportunity to receive technologies and developing capability to apply them to numerous industries to modify and adjust

**Exhibit 12-1**
**A Proactive Growth Strategy**

Organizing to create and maintain public order, construct and maintain infrastructure, organize and staff schools, deliver health care services.

Being a wise borrower, making sure that what has been borrowed is funneled as investment in factories, equipment and housing.

Developing the conditions to enhance entrepreneurship and emergence of learning organizations.

Creating opportunity to receive technologies and ability to modify and adjust them for local needs.

Establishing partnerships, networks and trading blocs to optimize the involvement in globalization.

Developing proactive growth strategies by emphasizing strengths and eliminating weaknesses.

Establishing an equitable system to distribute the benefits of globalization.

Accelerating growth by greater involvement in globalization and generating wealth and consumer value.

*Source:* Adapted and revised from Thurow (1999) and Samli (2001).

them to satisfy local needs is the next step. However, it must be kept in mind that without the first three steps, this fourth one cannot possibly materialize.

Once technologies are transferred successfully, companies from emerging markets can go through the steps discussed in Chapters 10 and 11 to establish partnerships, networks and trading blocs so that they can optimally be involved in the globalization process and receive all the benefits of globalization with little or no concern about being left out or being marginalized.

The next step in Exhibit 12–1 is perhaps the most critical for a country's future. Having the technology, having the entrepreneurial and learning capabilities and even having proper partnerships, networks or trading blocs does not represent the whole picture. It is very critical to develop growth strategies that go beyond short-run trade and to explore creation of the best economic conditions for the country, the region or the industry during the foreseeable future. More is said about this topic in Chapter 13.

If the society wants to play a role in and receive the full benefits of globalization, it will have to establish an equitable system so that the benefits of this involvement can be distributed equitably. This orientation will generate more support for global involvement rather than resistance. At the writing of this book, about 100,000 young people are expected to demonstrate in front of the International Monetary Fund headquarters in Washington, DC. Such actions, particularly in Third World countries, not only can get out of hand and become major confrontations or riots, but also become very disruptive in international business negotiations and economic plans that otherwise would be quite beneficial. Equity in distributing the benefits can be accomplished a number of different ways. Some of these are discussed in the next section.

The final step in Exhibit 12–1 is accelerating economic growth by greater involvement in globalization and generating wealth and consumer value. This last step represents the cumulative impact of the previous seven steps. Such an overall proactive growth strategy is not very easy to construct, but with proper leadership and political stability, this can be accomplished. The important point is to have visionary idealists in both private and public sectors who are willing to work for the good of the country as well as for their own well-being.

**Exhibit 12-2**
**Some Alternatives to Distributing the Benefits of Globalization**

| System of Distribution | Proposed Impact |
| --- | --- |
| • Progressive income tax | Utilization of extra revenues to improve infrastructure, education, etc. |
| • Tax benefits for enterprises that employ more people | Reduced unemployment and improved economic conditions |
| • Additional education and training programs financed by global successes | Improved skills of the labor force |
| • Improved supply of convenience products with improved quality | Improved quality of life of the poor and lower middle class |

## A BETTER JOB IN DISTRIBUTING BENEFITS

The proactive growth strategy discussed above does not do enough to explain how the benefits of globalization and the results of wealth-generation are to be distributed more reasonably or equitably so that some regions, groups or countries can avoid being marginalized. But it must also be understood that stopping marginalization also means economic improvement. If, for instance, an industrialized country conducting business with a Third World country has succeeded in making a major contribution to the economy of that Third World country, then the Third World country has become a better customer. It will, in return, buy more from the industrialized country. If more and more countries are economically advanced, world markets will be greater. The economic advancement is at least partially related to better distribution of the wealth generated. Thus, distributing the benefits of globalization has far-reaching effects to all parties concerned.

Just how can the benefits of globalization be distributed? Exhibit 12–2 illustrates four alternatives that would fulfill the goal of better distribution of these benefits.

The first alternative deals with progressive income taxes. By means of such a taxation system, it is possible to generate extra revenues by governments that can be used to improve infrastructures or education systems. How much tax and how much progressivity are critical questions. The only proviso here is not to style initiative as exercising fairness. Other than that each case is based on its merits and, therefore, each case is likely to be different.

The second alternative is giving tax benefits to those businesses that employ more and new workers. Those businesses benefiting from globalization share the benefits with these additional workers.

The third alternative is additional education and training programs to be financed by global successes. In other words, those firms that experience global success will make extra contributions to the education system so that the skills and knowledge base of the labor force will improve. This is a more indirect approach than the previous alternative. However, it could be farther reaching in terms of impacting larger groups of workers and benefiting more sectors or regions.

Finally, the fourth alternative shown in Exhibit 12–2 deals with more orderly adjustments in the market. As Vietnam enters the globalization process, the rumors are such that the costs of essentials such as bread or apparel have increased outrageously. One way toward equitable distribution of the economic benefits of globalization is making sure that the cost of living will not spiral upward. Improved economic riches should, at least partially, provide standard goods and services that are used by the poor and the lower middle classes at reasonable prices, with ever-improving quality.

It is clear that there could be other approaches. Exhibit 12–2 is to be used as an illustrative alternative rather than an exhaustive list. Furthermore, any one of the four alternatives in the exhibit can be implemented one at a time or all together. Similarly, they can be implemented differently in each country. One size in these issues *never* fits all.

## DEVELOPING THE NATIONAL ECONOMY BY DEFENSE

Developing a proactive defense mechanism goes way beyond Exhibit 12–1. The direction of the proactive growth strategy is very difficult to decide. Some countries, such as Singapore, Hong Kong, Chile and China, have used different pathways and performed reasonably well. There is no one perfect way. All pathways have pluses and minuses. This is partially due to the conceptualization of the pathway itself and partially due to its implementation. Kotler et al. (1997) have presented a very good discussion of alternative pathways to development.

One of the alternatives this author subscribes to is import substitutions. If the country does not have some of the most important ingredients of the prevailing economic activity, something very shocking can take place. After the first petroleum problem, which was at least partially caused by OPEC, in the early 1970s a number of countries experienced internal revolutions, military takeovers and other very dramatic events. Because of the energy shortage, caused by petroleum supply deficiency, some countries' industrial activity fell to a shocking 10 percent capacity. That created waves of unemployment, hunger and frustration. Countries were caught without alternatives. They could not switch, say, from petroleum to hydroelectric power. They could not run their motor vehicles with alcohol or electricity. They could not be engaged in a soft-landing rather than an all-devastating economic impact.

Globalization can become too much of a dependency on international sources or resources. It is critical for all countries, from the United States to Uganda, to develop other key alternatives to energy utilization, to raw material shortages, to knowledge inadequacies, among others. Here import substitution is critical. The Japanese Ministry of International Trade and Industry always prioritized the country's dependency from most to least and targeted some industries to substitute imports.

For small, poor countries that suffer from an acute shortage of foreign exchanges and become very dependent on certain imports, developing a proactive defense mechanism that takes import substitution seriously can be advisable. In such cases, substituting imports with domestically developed industries and products (if at all feasible) means more than exports because domestic development of industries would create a multiplier effect in economic growth. Under such circumstances, the foreign exchange saved from substituting such a necessity can be used on more futuristic projects such as bringing into the country new and promising industries, developing research and/ or an education tradition.

Developing an import-substitution-oriented proactive defense mechanism, in addition to the key considerations above, has at least three critical areas that need to be taken extremely seriously: exam-

ining the key weaknesses, prioritizing the needs proactively and generating corrective action.

Every country must be able to identify where it is most vulnerable,
be it the food supply, medication, energy or information, to name a
few. The countries that are not cognizant of their extreme dependencies or major weaknesses may not be able to survive. How these
weaknesses are identified may be accomplished differently. Countries
may have different ways of assessing their economic strengths and
weaknesses.

Prioritizing needs is not the same as prioritizing them proactively.
What is meant here by "proactively" is that if the importance of needs
or dependencies is based on the present rather than the future, that
is not proactive. For example, the United States has known its dependency on petroleum. This dependency is becoming more serious
as time goes by. If the problem was temporarily solved by digging
holes in Alaska, it is not proactive if the country tries to solve the
problem by developing alternative energy sources that are futuristic
and/or proactive. Many developing countries face similar problems
that are very critical. This author believes that without a proactive
orientation and making provision for future development, countries
cannot benefit from globalization and avoid marginalization.

Proactive prioritization is critical, but the whole proactive defense
mechanism depends upon how and what corrective action is taken.
For instance, South Korea dwelled upon an export-oriented industrialization. Singapore utilized a high-tech and service development
approach. China moved from agriculture to major infrastructure development (Kotler et al. 1997). These countries and others have designed and utilized proactive defense strategies and corrected their
weaknesses as they developed their economies in a proactive manner.

## AGAIN, THE BEST DEFENSE IS AN OFFENSE

It is posited here that a proactive growth strategy can get a country
not only to participate in globalization gainfully, but also to prevent
itself from being marginalized. Developing and implementing a successful proactive growth strategy calls for seeking and receiving approval from the partners, networks and participants in trading blocs.
With their help and approval, and by going through the steps identified in Exhibit 12–1, Third World countries can develop reasonably
tightly designed and even more tightly administered plans. Success of

these plans is beneficial not only to all those involved and participating in these economic activities but, in the long run, to the whole world.

## SUMMARY

A defense mechanism against marginalization is necessary for the Third World or emerging countries. This defense mechanism needs to be proactive and must have multiple dimensions. It boils down to the fact that these countries must learn to participate in globalization successfully and distribute the gain from this participation equitably. For a good defense mechanism to be effective, some degree of political stability is necessary. The Four Tigers have been successful at least partially because of such a stability.

The chapter refers to a successful defense mechanism based on proactivity. Countries must develop proactive growth strategies that will enable them to take full advantage of globalization while preventing marginalization. This is why the best defense is an offense.

A proactive growth strategy of eight steps is presented in the chapter: (1) organizing and maintaining public order, infrastructure, schools and healthcare services; (2) being a wise borrower and investing in factories, equipment and housing; (3) developing and enhancing entrepreneurship and learning organizations; (4) creating opportunity to receive, modify and adjust technologies; (5) establishing partnerships, networks and trading blocs; (6) developing any proactive growth strategies by emphasizing strengths and eliminating weaknesses; (7) establishing an equitable system to distribute the benefits of globalization; and (8) accelerating growth by greater involvement in globalization and generating wealth and consumer value.

Item seven above is considered very critical. The chapter presents four alternatives to the distribution of the benefits of globalization: (1) progressive income tax, (2) tax benefits for enterprises to employ more people, (3) additional education and training programs financed by global successes, and (4) improved supply of convenience products with further improved quality.

## REFERENCES

Friedman, Thomas L. (2000). *The Lexus and the Olive Tree*. New York: Anchor Books.

Kotler, Philip, Jatusripitak, Somkid, and Maesincee, Suvit (1997). *The Marketing of Nations.* New York: The Free Press.
Samli, A. Coskun (2001). *Empowering the American Consumer.* Westport, CT: Quorum Books.
Thurow, Lester C. (1999). *Building Wealth.* New York: HarperCollins Publishers.

# Chapter 13

# Strategic Plan That Works

Developing a proactive defense mechanism is critical but does not imply its total success. In fact nothing would guarantee a total success. Perhaps this is why the proactive defense mechanism must be treated as a strategic plan and efforts must be made so that it works. When the Four Tigers implemented their strategies, perhaps they did or did not have a contingency plan. However, as the globalization process accelerates, the electronic herd (Friedman 2000) starts moving toward the country.

There is not much time to evaluate the proactive defense mechanism. The country could be run over by the electronic herd quickly. Thus, a strategic plan needs to be in place. This is a game plan that will protect the country from the electronic herd by perhaps becoming part of it. This is not at all saying that the country needs to be isolated so that it will be protected from the potential harm by the electronic herd. On the contrary, it means that the country will take advantage of the situation and benefit from it.

## THE NEED FOR FAST DEVELOPMENT

In an earlier book, Thurow (1992) spoke about international trade. He suggested that international trade in the second half of the 20th century was a win/win situation. Virtually all parties engaged in global trading benefited from it. However, he suggested that in the 21st century, it is going to be a win/lose situation. This can easily be connected to Friedman's electronic herd metaphor. If the electronic herd is going to run over the country, there hardly will be a win/win scenario. Understanding the situation clearly, reversing the damage to be caused by the electronic herd and quickly converting the win/lose situation to win/win is necessary. Developing and implementing the strategic plan without delay is extremely critical if the country wants to benefit from globalization without being marginalized.

## STRATEGIC POSTURING

Exhibit 13–1 illustrates two key dimensions to be carefully considered as the strategic plan is constructed and implemented: proactivity or reactivity dimension, and the offensive or defensive dimension. It is maintained here that if these two dimensions are put together carefully, they will provide the most appropriate strategy posturing. The upper left quadrant of the two-by-two matrix, shown in Exhibit 13–1, illustrates the most appropriate strategic posture. Here countries, regions, industries or even companies are being proactive and displaying this proactivity with an offensive plan of action. For instance, this author believes the Four Tigers of Asia have had such a strategic orientation. They took early advantage of transferred technology and developed ambitious global marketing programs and competed vigorously in the world markets. Most important, they succeeded by taking full advantage of globalization.

Even though the country is not proactive enough by engaging in an offensive, at least not fully, it is benefiting from offensive globalization. Perhaps the current stature and the performance of the People's Republic of China can be labeled this way. This is the upper right quadrant of Exhibit 13–1.

The lower left quadrant indicates a proactive defense. A fast defensive mechanism to protect the country without much benefit from globalization does not represent a progressive posture. The country, by acting swiftly, is keeping globalization out, but this is not altogether beneficial. Perhaps Iran or Syria may be considered in this group of countries that are utilizing such a strategy.

Finally, there are many Third World countries that are not fast in the defense area, so they are being marginalized. They are not re-

**Exhibit 13-1**
**Stategic Posturing**

Offensive  Proactive                                                Reactive

| | |
|---|---|
| Most effective strategy posture. Optimize benefits of globalization and minimize marginalization by preempting it. | Some benefit from globalization. Taking strong offensive position when the marginalization is felt. |
| Fast defense mechanism to protect the country without much benefit from globalization. Holding ground. | Typical behavior pattern of many Third World countries. No benefits of globalization and no defense toward marginalization until too late. |

Defensive

ceiving any benefit from globalization either. They do not have much defense as the marginalization continues and advances. Somalia and Sudan may be considered in this group that is represented by the lower right quadrant.

## GLOBAL OR NATIONAL

It can be observed from Exhibit 13–1 that the countries that are more on the offensive are global. They try to participate in the globalization process in such a way that they will not be marginalized. On the other hand, defensive countries are more likely to be national. They mostly defend their national economies by trying to keep globalization out. Is it possible to combine these two approaches and be truly successful? In many ways, this is the major theme of this book, and many of its chapters make this kind of thinking possible and this kind of action plausible. But, both offensively and defensively, countries need certain apparatus in their possession and certain capabilities within their spectrum of skills. For instance, without production capabilities that imply having up-to-date factories, without proper logistics systems that enable efficient handling and movement of raw materials as well as finished goods and without good environmental protection, countries cannot be on the offensive, nor can they defend themselves.

A compromised position here is called "glocalizing," which implies both being global and adjusting it to local conditions (Friedman 2000).

## THE BENEFITS OF BEING UP-TO-DATE

In Chapters 2, 5 and 6 it was argued that one of the most important flows that facilitates globalization and accelerates it is technology flow. In the process of technologies flowing from one country to another throughout the world, the Third World countries have a good chance of receiving the technology successfully. With the exception of a special situation discussed in Chapter 6 in conjunction with piracy, the typical flow is to less-developed countries from the industrial world. When these countries receive the technology, they can develop the most cutting-edge production facilities. This kind of opportunity did not exist until the 1970s. Having the most cutting-edge manufacturing facilities, above all, makes it very attractive from a world trade perspective. This is because manufacturing facilities in the developed world are already there and are one generation older— they are no longer cutting-edge facilities. The older facilities are not nearly as productive as the cutting-edge facilities. Furthermore, in developing countries labor is cheaper, and if the technology is manipulated to suit the local needs, then the quality can be better.

Exhibit 13–2 illustrates how a successfully transferred technology functions. With the most up-to-date technology comes a high level of productivity along with increased quality. Additionally, increased efficiency generates reductions on cost. All of these are further reinforced by lower wage rates. The end result is what Hong Kong and Singapore have experienced. They successfully received the cutting-edge technologies along with their relatively low-cost labor. They have become powerful competitors in world markets. One of the most important points in Exhibit 13–2 is what this author calls "spill-over." As new industries emerge, they directly or indirectly influence many other industries that have been there for a while. The vitality of the new and up-to-date industries spills over onto other industries and revitalizes them. This process, as a whole, accelerates economic

**Exhibit 13-2**
**Being Up-to-Date**

growth. As growth is experienced, a proactive defense mechanism is considered fully functional. Here countries are experiencing economic growth through globalization.

## CONCERTED EFFORTS AND CONCERTED WILL

To develop and implement a working strategic plan requires a concerted effort on the part of the government. The industry and certain companies that are involved, or likely to become involved, must make an effort to work with the government to create a fully beneficial situation. Here the government creates the proper conditions for companies to receive technologies successfully and put them to good use. This is what took place in the Asian Four Tigers, but is not taking place in many developing countries. This kind of deliberate and focused effort cannot exist unless there is a concerted will to accomplish what needs to be done.

The old adage "best defense is an offense" was used in the previous chapter. However, there are two diametrically opposing positions here *defense-offense* versus *offense-offense*. In other words, should the Third World country start with a defensive posture? This could be construed as offensive against marginalization. But it is critical to identify where the best advantages lie and what kinds of priorities need to be established.

To be engaged in offense-offense, conditions must be right. Having production and distribution capabilities and, prior to these, the entrepreneurial spirit, is necessary. It is critical, therefore, that in a poor country where marginalization is imminent, the conditions must be there for at least a *defense-offense* situation. From there the country can reach out and globalize by means of *offense-offense*. This offense-offense implies that the country is not only resisting marginalization by moving into the global arena with much zeal, but using the globalization process faster and more efficiently than many others.

Perhaps a most important activity in constructing a strategic plan that works is to use some version of SWOT (strengths, weaknesses, opportunities and threats) analysis that will enable the country to *prioritize, activate, implement and evaluate* the strategic plan that represents a proactive defense mechanism. These four activities need to be explored.

*Prioritize*: Through SWOT analysis, a number of possible opportunities for the country emerge. It is critical to prioritize these according to their potential contribution to the economy and according to their possible global impact. One important criterion can be in exploring the alternative which is most likely to help globalization of the country, industry or firm.

*Activate*: Once prioritization occurs, the best-case scenario is activated. That means, as planned, the project is readied for implementation. Activation here implies detailed plans and blueprints before the project is implemented.

*Implement*: After it is activated, the project needs to be implemented. Such project implementation would accelerate the country's successful participation in globalization.

*Evaluate*: Implementation and evaluation go hand-in-hand. If the project is not successful, it is necessary to find out why and if the situation can be rectified. Learning from the evaluation process also would make other future projects more successful.

Dealing with the strengths of the country and its resources exerts a special pressure on developing a strategic plan that works. A resource-based internationalization model can be very strong if the country's resources are objectively evaluated (Sharma 2001). This would be the "S" in SWOT analysis. It is quite possible that weaknesses of the country may outstrip strengths in such a way that the best approach to the development of a workable strategic plan may start with some major import substitution or weakness evaluation. If, for instance, the country is heavily petroleum-dependent and petroleum prices are going up very fast, in order for the country to generate exportable products, it may proceed toward developing another type of energy and substitute this very vital import.

By the same token, opportunities and threats need to be analyzed so that the developing country can make a viable move. It is critical that the country's strengths and opportunities are matched.

## THE SECOND HALF OF THE OFFENSIVE

In the above case, without *defense-offense*, the country will have difficulty reaching *offense-offense*. In dealing with this aspect of a workable strategic plan, it is critical to emphasize one point: Being or becoming global does not mean not being local. In some sense, this is similar to "glocalization." Friedman (2000) defines this concept as the ability of a culture to absorb influences from other cultures as long as they naturally fit into the existing culture. When the technology is successfully transferred, the receiving country, as it becomes global, also maintains its local nature.

But there is more. The Third World country, in the process of developing a strategic plan that works, must make sure that whatever it does has dual benefits. The activities must not only facilitate the country's globalization opportunities but simultaneously also the development of the domestic economy. For instance, if the country is planning to export textiles and develop its logistics infrastructure toward this end, it doesn't mean that the developed infrastructure cannot be used for certain domestic economic activity. In other words, when the country builds its logistic infrastructure, it can make sure that the transportation, storage, communication, energy supplies and other related infrastructure can enhance both the country's globalization and the domestic economy simultaneously. This multipurpose usage of logistics infrastructure provides reassurance about economic progress. If globalization does not work, domestic economic growth can be achieved. Thus the country, in a slight twist from Friedman, globalizes in its strategic offensive and counteracts the electronic herd.

## SWOT ANALYSIS APPLIED

In dealing with SWOT analysis in an attempt to develop a workable strategic plan, two categories of information are used, internal factors and external factors (Czinkota, Kotabe and Mercer 1997). It must be reiterated that using such an analysis for a company is not much

**Exhibit 13-3**
**Applying SWOT Analysis**

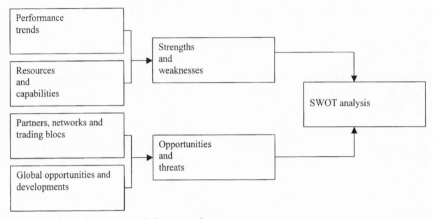

*Source:* Adapted and revised from Czinkota et al. (1997).

different from using the same analytic model for a country. Exhibit 13–3 illustrates how SWOT analysis can be used. As seen in the exhibit, there are four sets of analyses.

*Performance trends*: The country's domestic and international activities are analyzed in an effort to determine its well-performing sectors versus its sectors that are performing less than adequately. Performance trends can easily illustrate where more resources are likely to pay off. For instance, such trends may show that the country's traditional export, say rubber, is on the decline, while its international activity related to computer components is growing very noticeably.

*Resources and capabilities*: The country's resources and capabilities are measured against the trends. Critical decisions need to be made as to which resources may be utilized to cultivate which capabilities further. This author visited Malaysia when the country had more job openings in computer component and other related high-tech areas than it could possibly fill. Such situations indicate strengths and weaknesses. But adequate planning for the future must be further carried out, since opportunities are not a fixed sets of facts.

*Partners, networks and trading blocs*: If the country wants to further its involvement in, say, computer components and other electronic supplies, it will have to work very closely with its partners, networks and trading blocs. These must all be functional and supportive so that the country can become more global. Assuming good and mutually beneficial relationships, countries, regions or industries will have to map out continuation, expansion or variations of these relationships in the direction of greater benefits for all. This is where experts maintain that never, in the economic history of recent times, have countries been more economically interdependent (Ghauri 2001).

*Global developments*: Analyzing global developments within the context of SWOT analysis finally puts together opportunities and threats. New global developments lead in the direction of new opportunities and new threats. Such analysis takes the whole set of considerations back to performance and resource examination. It is therefore critical to emphasize the fact that such SWOT analysis is an ongoing activity and needs to be revised and updated very regularly if not continuously.

Thus, the second half of the offensive is based on carefully developed SWOT analysis. Clearly, when the workable strategic plan is constructed, it is critical to make sure that it is detailed according to characteristics of a marketing strategy dealing with the product, promotion, price and place where the products are stored, distributed and sold. Here, still, the countries will have to determine the weight they will put on internal versus external orientation and pursuant activities (Capon and Hulbert 2000).

It must be noted that SWOT analysis is not the only way. Here this approach is shown as an example as to what countries can do if they want to defend themselves from the ills of marginalization, by using strong offensive moves.

Other microplanning techniques such as portfolio planning and marketing audit analysis can also work in the same direction. The essence of thinking here is that the country follows a carefully planned and implemented strategy that will improve its participation in and its benefits from the globalization process. This, by definition, preempts marginalization that may otherwise take place. It must be reiterated here that utilizing microplanning techniques, for national performance, have not been utilized widely. However, this is a very important approach to developing workable strategic plans. In the past, countries resorted to macroplanning techniques that did not work very well. The demise of the USSR is at least partially due to rather dysfunctional macroplanning techniques.

## WHERE THERE IS A WILL

Concerted efforts require concerted will. A logical continuation of such thinking is that the country, the elite, the government officials, the industrialists and perhaps, above all, the populace want to develop the country and its economy, and they are united in this direction. There are ways of accomplishing this goal. It is critical that all of these parties play a critical role in a country. They must be aware of the goals and must give their consent to the strategic plans that are in the making.

Here it is critical to repeat that, for a Third World country, what is good for its economic posture to become more global could also be good for its home front. These two must not be totally separated nor should they be opposed to each other. Thus, developing international capabilities along with domestic economic development, or "killing two birds with one stone," should be the goal. Such an orientation is synergistic, and the conditions do not represent a zero-sum game. In other words, carefully emphasizing domestic development along with globalization activity rather than emphazing one against the other will bring more and greater economic results. Here domestic and global together will add up to more than the sum total. If and when the globalization activity is powerfully implemented, then the marginalization danger will be avoided.

## SUMMARY

Starting with Chapter 8 and continuing on with subsequent chapters of this book, we have argued that there is more to not trading and being marginalized as the global pressures mount. It has been maintained that a proactive defense mechanism is needed.

In this chapter, the workings of such a strategic and proactive defense mechanism are developed into a strategy. It is mentioned here that such a strategic posturing may vary from proactive to reactive and from offensive to defensive. If at all possible, strategic posturing should go in the direction of proactive and offensive.

In planning and implementing such a strategy, being up-to-date is extremely critical. Many emerging countries are not in a position to develop technologies from scratch on their own. But they could benefit substantially if they could facilitate a successful transferal of the technology. The receiving country must be capable of using this up-to-date technology, creating high productivity along with increased quality and, finally, must be able to take advantage of increased efficiency by reducing costs. Such orientation does not merely stay with one industry alone; it spills over to other industries as well.

These efforts, however, require concerted will on the part of the country as a whole. If the government, the elite, the managerial group and the populace don't realize what is happening and don't participate in these far-reaching activities together, very little can be accomplished. Finally, in developing a strategic plan that works, countries are advised to use microplanning tools to plan and implement macrostrategies. One such tool, SWOT analysis, is presented as it applies to the global considerations that the country is facing. In order to implement SWOT analyses, the chapter presents, a brief discussion of four specific analytical activities: (1) performance trends; (2) resources and capabilities; (3) partners, networks and trading blocs; and (4) global developments.

## REFERENCES

Capon, Noel and Hulbert, James M. (2000). *Marketing Management in The 21st Century*. Upper Sadde River, NJ: Prentice Hall.

Czinkota, Michael R., Kotabe, Masaaki and Mercer, David (1997). *Marketing Management*. Cambridge, MA: Blackwell Publishers.

Friedman, Thomas L. (2000). *The Lexus and the Olive Tree*. New York: Anchor Books.

Ghauri, Pervez N. (2001). "Using Cooperative Strategies to Compete in a Changing World." in C. P. Rao (ed.), *Globalization and Its Managerial Implications*. Westport, CT: Quorum Books.

Sharma, D. Deo (2001). "A Resource-Based Model of the Internationalization Process of the Firm," in C. P. Rao (ed.), *Globalization and Its Managerial Implications*. Westport, CT: Quorum Books.

Thurow, Lester C. (1992). *Head to Head*. New York: William Morrow.

# Chapter 14

# Future Outlook and a Research Agenda

Friedman (2000) talks about stabilizing the globalization process by democratization. But, unfortunately, democracies are not well-established and are not stable enough. As he talks about globalization being Darwinism on steroids, he makes the case against democratization. This author discussed elsewhere (Samli 2001) that there are two democracies: political democracy which means one person, one vote, and economic democracy that entails one dollar, one vote. But it appears that economic democracy is gaining ground over political democracy in the sense that the domestic U.S. economy is becoming more and more top-heavy in that the rich have been getting richer and the poor, poorer. Add into such a situation the concept of Darwinism on steroids, and the whole world economy becomes more unstable as have-nots become have-nothings and haves become have-mores.

Unchecked as it is, without any global laws or regulations, globalization is on a dangerous course. If we analyze any war in history, we see a critical economic dimension based on inequalities. The way globalization is functioning at the present time is more of a global imperialism of the dollar than a fair economic activity that will benefit all participants.

## CAN THERE BE A GLOBAL CAPITALISM FREE AND FAIR?

When downsizing, wage cutting, moving factories to low-wage and environmentally loose countries, maximum wages are maximized, minimum wages are kept to a minimum and other chaotic changes are all considered to be victories for democracy. In the United States, and when such values are transported to many countries that have very little democratic tradition and very economically divided societies, there is a major problem. The problem is exacerbated by the fact that there are no rules, regulations or authorities that will balance globalization. Unchecked, globalization will make things much worse. It will be difficult to call expanding capitalism fair. It is maintained that global capitalism (or globalization) cannot remain free if it is not fair. When the Mongolians pirated the riches of China, that was not fair. When Hitler took all the riches of Europe by force, that was not fair. When globalization plays extreme favoritism toward the rich around the world, that is not fair either. What is needed is a globalization process that is sustainable.

Clearly, sustainable globalization is extremely desirable if it is based on fairness. It will have to distribute its benefits among all participants. Thus, in this book, a strong position is taken not against globalization but for distributing its benefits more equitably. In fact, without globalization there may not be any benefits to distribute.

## THERE ARE NOT MANY ALTERNATIVES

It must be emphasized dramatically that if all the world markets share the benefits of globalization and become full beneficiaries of the globalization movement, then there will be no reason to think of pirates surrounding the extreme rich or sheep dogs (or tanks) attacking the electronic herd. Sustainable globalization is a major goal that we must aim at and work for relentlessly. Although in its present form globalization may not be doing much good for many in the world, it is the only opportunity for the poor nations to enter the world's mainstream economic progress. It is through globalization that poor countries will learn to produce economic riches for their populations.

At no place in this book has there been an argument for a worldwide superpower. In fact, it is doubtful that such an organization could bridge the gap between the rich and the poor. We have experiences to that effect. After almost 300 years, Tennessee and Ken-

Exhibit 14-1
Globalization without Marginalization

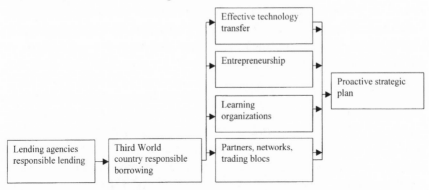

tucky are not very high in the economic spectrum of the United States. Poorer members of the European Union are still poor, if not poorer. It is clear that economically well-off countries through globalization are treating the world's economic riches as a zero-sum game in that someone must lose so they get rich. As a result, at the beginning of the 21st century, we do not have evil empires or dictatorships of significance, but we do have a fast-growing capitalist imperialism. The power of the dollar is terrorizing many poor countries, and globalization is accentuating this problem. In short, global capitalism at this time is not democratic enough. It cannot be sustained in a desirable manner.

## GLOBALIZATION WILL GO ON

Unless a calamity such as a world war occurs, globalization, the single most important economic phenomenon of our times, will continue. It is not stoppable. What needs to be understood is that countries can be full participants in the globalization process without becoming marginalized. This book puts bits and pieces together to construct a proactive defense mechanism in the form of a strategic plan that works. With such a plan, countries that are currently being marginalized can become full beneficiaries of the globalization process.

Exhibit 14-1 illustrates the key elements of the strategic plan that is constructed throughout the book. The whole process begins with a fair lending process. Unlike Friedman (2000), who makes a case for bad-borrowing countries, it is critical to realize that the lender has the upper hand. In other words, there are bad-lending countries and they play a critical role in the capital flow around the world. As discussed in Chapter 7, many countries are put in a straightjacket that fits all. A defense mechanism cannot be activated if the borrowing country is forced to have its hands tied because, deep down, the lender wants to have its money back in full and also would like to get the highest possible return. The lender's best interest and the borrower's best interest clash right at the outset. Exhibit 14–1 illustrates a compromise where the lender will have responsible lending policies and the borrower will borrow wisely. This is the starting point of the whole process, and is a necessary condition. If there are no funds and if the available funds are not being used for the necessary projects, the whole defense mechanism cannot get started.

In Exhibit 14–1, effective technology transfer leads to the next series of activities. It is certainly up to the receiving country to take the necessary steps. Perhaps an international commission can help these countries to construct their strategic plans. As discussed in Chapters 8 and 9, the emerging country that wants to protect itself from being stampeded by the electronic herd (Friedman 2000) must facilitate the emergence of an atmosphere supportive of entrepreneuship and learning organizations. Again, as discussed in Chapters 10 and 11, emerging countries must develop partnerships, must participate in networks and must become a part of trading blocs.

## GLOBALIZATION CAN REACH FURTHER

Reiterating one of the key points of this book, as long as globalization is allowed to continue as a rich country's game while spreading global imperialism, there will be a worsening gap between the have-nothings (a very large group) and have-mores (a relatively small group). Expanded participation in globalization is beneficial to the whole world. Among other things, it will make it less likely for future world terrorists to emerge. It has been said that to alleviate the poverty of hundreds of millions of people in the developing world, globalization should be looked at as a remedy (Catlaui 2001). But as stated in the Preface, not the G7 convention but a G191 convention must take place. In other words, all countries must participate in a discussion of the world's economic future.

Thus, globalization is a major hope, but only if it can reach further. One of the most important provisos for this statement lies in a more equitable distribution of the benefits of globalization. In order for globalization to reach out and touch all, a research agenda must be developed and followed carefully. The following section proposes such an agenda. It must be kept in mind that this is not an exhaustive but only a suggestive list of topics and necessary future analysis. Two closely related areas are left out of our discussion in this book. First environmental responsibility is not discussed in detail because it is a very important issue within itself and many books and articles already have been written about it. Many companies from emerging markets may not realize the importance of environmental responsibility. Furthermore, under the pressures of cost cutting stemming from outsourcing Western firms, these Third World firms may cause more pollution that can endanger the future of our planet Earth. This is an issue that must be taken separately and critically.

The second area not covered in this book is the broad issue of cultural change. Globalization creates cultural exchanges which inevitably lead to cultural change. Traditionalists in many cultures are opposed to such changes. However, cultural exchanges can provide new ways of thinking and new solutions to old problems. This is an important area that needs to be explored further in a separate effort.

## A RESEARCH AGENDA

Exhibit 14–2 identifies five research areas which this author thinks are important in the area of globalization. Perhaps the most important of these is developing a fairness doctrine. Globalization and the related four flows (see Chapter 1) cannot be left totally unchecked. Countries that benefit from globalization must be evaluated carefully, and adjustments should be made quickly if the results are not satisfactory.

Accomplishing better networking possibilities is critical not only for important strategic alliances to get started but also to perform in favor of globalization. Such proactivity is beneficial to all parties involved. Identifying the parties that are willing to participate, putting them in touch with each other and seeing to it that information will flow smoothly among them is important for the future growth and development of the world.

How to put together proactive strategic plans that will defend countries against marginalization and will make it possible for them to benefit from globalization is the essence of this book. However, such strategies are not fixed and do not come in one size. It is necessary to explore different strategic alternatives and decide which one

172 An Equitable, Sustainable Globalization

**Exhibit 14-2**
**A Research Agenda**

| Topics | Expected outcome |
| --- | --- |
| Developing a Fairness Doctrine | Evaluating progress of countries separately and devising new approaches if needed. |
| Better Networking Possibilities | Facilitating more partnering and returning for faster and better results. |
| Developing More Creative Strategies | Making sure that proactive strategic plans are very suitable to each country's needs. |
| How to Transfer Technologies | Obtaining better results from successfully transferred technologies. |
| Should There be Limits? | Understanding that excessive profits and unchecked behavior can create dire results. |

is most suitable for the country and how it will be implemented. Much research is needed in these critical areas.

Technology transfer is one of the most critical features of globalization. Without it, progress cannot be spread and globalization cannot yield benefits for all participants. Less-developed countries must welcome new technologies, learn to use them and become capable to adjust or modify them. Acceptance of new technologies is not automatic. It requires much research information to understand the workings of a successful technology transfer (Samli 1985). This is one key area that helped most of the newly industrialized societies. They not only developed industries but joined the globalization process in many ways, such as trade, sourcing, international finance and the like. Technologies must be transferred faster in an environmentally responsible fashion, and there are many ways of improving technology transfer.

Finally one must ask if what Friedman (2000) called Darwinism on steroids or the electronic herd should function altogether freely. When globalization yields money in the form of profits, which is good as a motivation for others to enter and participate, there must be a question, to what extent? How much of this profit is fair, and how much of it needs to be shared so that others can participate in the process? At the beginning of the book we stated that those who have are becoming have-mores and those who are have-nots are becoming have-nothings. The key question here is whether there are some limits. What needs to be done so that the globalization process can create a more equitable picture and fill in the gap between the have-mores and have-nothings? What needs to be done? And how do we go about doing it? If we don't do anything, it will be unreasonable to hope that things will get better.

It is quite frightening to think that one day some country may find itself surrounded with a bunch of pirates who don't have anything to lose because they don't have anything. These pirates will make the rich country totally miserable.

## PROGRESS, PROGRESS AND MORE PROGRESS

The world is at a crossroads. Although the IMF, the U.S. Treasury and fund managers are all asking Third World countries what they are doing to improve their financial systems, what are the inflows and outflows of money to and from their countries (Friedman 2000), these questions are not enough. First, the problems cannot be solved by money alone and, second, the IMF and others must also be asked to discover what they are doing for these countries that is wrong and must be corrected. Much more progress is needed in trade, in the industrialization process, in generating more equitable distribution of income and in creating more good jobs. In short, we need progress. Could globalization deliver that needed progress if it is totally unchecked? Unfortunately I think that is quite unlikely. But I also think that globalization, or shall I say "guided globalization," does have the solution. If globalization is used responsibly and as a tool to improve the world economy as a whole, it has a tremendous potential. It can reverse marginalization and benefit all. After all, the world we save is our own world, and there is only one of its kind.

## REFERENCES

Catlaui, Maria Livanos (2001). "Globalization Holds the Key to Ending World Poverty," *International Chamber of Commerce*, May 16.

Friedman, Thomas (2000). *The Lexus and the Olive Tree*. New York: Anchor Books.

Samli, A. Coskun (1985). *Technology Transfer*. Westport, CT: Quorum Books.

# Selected Bibliography

Ajami, Riad and Khambata, Dara (1991). "Global Strategic Alliances: The New Transnationals," *Journal of Global Marketing*, No. 1 and 2, 55–68.

Allee, Verna (2000). "Reconfiguring the Value Network," *The Journal of Business Strategy*, July/August, 36–39.

Anderson, Shirley C. (2000). "The Globally Competitive Firm: Functional Integration Value Chain Logistics, Global Marketing and Business College Strategic Support," *Competitiveness Review*, March 33–45.

Anthony, Robert (2000). "The Digital Divide Network," *Black Enterprise*, June, 11, 80.

Arbetter, Lisa (1994). "Intelligence Policy in a Changing World," *Security Management*, May, 39–42.

Atkinson, Glen (1999). "Developing Global Institutions: Lessons to be Learned from Regional Integration Experience," *Journal of Economic Issues*, June, 335–342.

Birdsall, Nancy (1998). "Life Is Unfair: Inequality in the World," *Foreign Policy*, Summer, 76–94.

Busenitz, Lowell W., Gomer, Carolina and Spencer, Jennifer W. (2000). "Country Institutional Profiles: Unlocking Entrepreneurial Phenomena," *Academy of Management Journal*, October, 994–1003.

*Business Week* (2001). "Global Capitalism," January 29.

Calantone, Roger J. and Zhao, Yushan Sam (2001). "Joint Ventures in China: A Comparative Study of Japanese, Korean and U.S.," *Journal of International Marketing*, January, 1–16.

Catlaui, Maria Livanos (2001). "Globalization Holds the Key to Ending World Poverty," *International Chamber of Commerce*, May 16.

Cheng, Lucie and Yang, Philip Q. (1998). "Global Interaction, Global Inequality and Migration of the Highly Trained to United States," *International Migration Review*, Fall, 626–645.

Crawford, Peter, Johnson, Kristen, Robb, James, and Sidebottom, Peter (1999). "Globalization of the Power and Light Industry," *McKinsey Quarterly*, Winter, 123–130.

Evenett, Simon J. (1999). "The World Trading System, the Road Ahead," *Finance and Development*, December, 22–28.

Friedman, Thomas (2000). *The Lexus and the Olive Tree*. New York: Anchor Books.

Garette, Bernard and Dussauge, Pierre (2000). "Alliances Versus Acquisitions: Choosing the Right Option," *European Management Journal*, February, 63–69.

Ghauri, Pervez N. (2001). "Using Cooperative Strategies to Compete in a Changing World," in C. P. Rao (ed.), *Globalization and Its Managerial Implications*. Westport, CT: Quorum Books.

Ghose, Ajit K. (2000). "Trade Liberalization, Employment and Global Inequality," *International Labor Review*, Autumn, 281–295.

Good, Mary Lowe (1999). "Technology and Trade," *Law and Policy in International Business*, Summer, 853–864.

Griswold, Daniel T. (1998). "Blessings and Burdens of Globalization," *World and I*, April, 30–36.

Harris, Jerry (1998). "Globalization and the Technological Transformation of Capitalism," *Race and Class*, October, 21–32.

Harsch, Ernest (1999). "Africa, Asia and Anxieties About Globalization," *Review of Political Economy*, March, 117–123.

Hill, Patrice (2000). "International Monetary Fund Defends Push for Globalization," Knight Ridder/Tribune Business News, April 12, 1–2.

Hitt, Michael A., Dacin, M. Tina, Levitas, Edward, Edhec, Jean-Luc Arregle and Borza, Anca (2000). "Partner Selection in Emerging and Developed Market Contexts: Resource-Based and Organizational Learning Perspectives," *Academy of Management Journal*, June, 449–467.

Hoffman, Thomas (2000). "Leaders: Education Key to Bridging Digital Divide," *Computer World*, September 11, 14–16.

Kotler, Philip, Jatusripitak, Somkid and Maesincee, Suvit (1997). *The Marketing of Nations*, New York: The Free Press.

Kraus, James R. (2000). "Andersen Consulting Study Throws Some Cold Water On Globalization Strategy," *American Banker*, February, 26, 36.

Lee, Sang M. and Peterson, Suzanne J. (2000). "Culture Entreperneurial Orientation and Global Competitiveness," *Journal of World Business*, Winter, 401–417.

Marcharzina, Klaus (2000). "Entrepreneurship on a Global Rise?" *Management International Review*, 3rd Quarter, 199–202.

McCormick, Richard D. (2000). "10 Myths About Globalization: Modern Civilization Through Trade To All," *Vital Speeches*, November 15, 69–74.

Moe, Michael J. (2001). "Creating Value Through Working with Others: Interorganizational Relationships," *The Academy of Management Executive*, February, 150–152.

National Counter Intelligence Center (1997). "1997 Annual Report to Congress on Foreign Economic Collection and Industrial Espionage," Annual Report to Congress, September, 1–16.

Ng, Francis and Yeats, Alexander (1997). "Open Economies Work Better! Did Africa's Protectionist Policies Cause Its Marginalization in World Trade?" *World Development*, No. 6, 889–904.

Peng, Mike W. and Shekshina, Stanislov V. (2001). "How Entrepreneurs Create Wealth in Transition Economies," *The Academy of Management Executives*, February, 95–110.

Rao, C. P. (2001). *Globalization and Its Managerial Implications*. Westport, CT: Quorum Books.

Rosen, George (2000). "Globalization, Growth and Marginalization," *Pacific Affairs*, Winter, 572.

Samli, A. Coskun (1985). *Technology Transfer: Geographic, Economic, Cultural and Technical Dimensions*. Westport, CT: Quorum Books.

Samli, A. Coskun (1992). *Social Responsibility in Marketing*. Westport, CT: Quorum Books.

Samli, A. Coskun (1996). *Information-Driven Marketing Decisions*. Westport, CT: Quorum Books.

Samli, A. Coskun (2001). *Empowering the American Consumer*. Westport, CT: Quorum Books.

Scott, Bruce R. (2001). "The Great Divide in the Global Village," *Foreign Affairs*, January–February, 160–171.

Smadja, Claude (1999). "Living Dangerously: We Need New International Mechanisms to Harness Globalization's Potential to Generate Prosperity," *Time*, February 22, 94.

Thyfault, Mary E. (2001). "Global Opportunities," *Information Week*, March 26, 65–70.

Wilber, Charles K. (1998). "Globalization and Democracy," *Journal of Economic Issues*, June, 465–470.

# Index

## About the Author

A. COSKUN SAMLI is Research Professor of Marketing and International Business at the University of North Florida, Jacksonville. Author or coauthor of more than 250 scholarly articles, 13 books and 30 monographs, he has been invited as a distinguished scholar to deliver papers at more than a dozen universities. He has lectured in countries around the world, is the cofounder and very active in the International Society for Quality of Life Studies (ISQOLS), serves on the review boards of seven major journals and is a Senior Fellow in the Academy of Marketing Science. Among his more recent books published by Quorum are: *Counterturbulence Marketing: A Proactive Strategy for Volatile Economic Times* (1993), *International Consumer Behavior: Its Impact on Marketing Strategy* (1995), *Information-Driven Marketing Decisions: Development of Strategic Information Systems* (1996), *Strategic Marketing for Success in Retailing* (1998), and *Empowering the American Consumer* (2001).